When STORY magazine devoted its entire issue for September-October, 1941 as an homage to Sherwood Anderson, it paid tribute to a writer acclaimed a... of America's foremost deline... ... life in the short story form, and a masterful reporter of the Depression Age. Significantly, the contributors were among the country's most noteworthy authors, including Waldo Frank, Gertrude Stein, Thomas Wolfe, Theodore Dreiser, Henry Miller, William Saroyan, Kenneth Patchen, Ben Hecht and Jesse Stuart in its roster.

An important nucleus of a burgeoning bibliography of critical estimates of Anderson's writings, the STORY issue, because of its perishable magazine format, was to become virtually unobtainable. Coincident with a re-awakened interest in all of his works, it was determined this was the appropriate time to reissue the HOMAGE in a more substantial and suitable binding. Included in this edition is a selection of unpublished Anderson letters written during the '30s. Finally, it was felt that the addition of a scarce essay, THE MODERN WRITER, issued in a limited edition back in 1925, would be of extra value and interest to the reader.

Homage to
Sherwood
Anderson

1876-1941

Sherwood Anderson at Ripshin Farm about 1939

Homage to Sherwood Anderson

1876-1941

Edited by
Paul P. Appel

PAUL P. APPEL, *Publisher*

MAMARONECK, N.Y.

1970

Library of Congress Catalog Card Number—77-105304

S.B.N. - 911858-02-4

Foreword

The idea behind the republication of this homage may be of sufficient interest to the reader to warrant this brief explanation. Shortly after the tragic death of Sherwood Anderson in March of 1941, STORY magazine asked some of the country's leading authors for their impression of Anderson, both as a writer and as a man, and devoted an entire issue in homage to his memory. Recognized as a major force in American literature during his lifetime, Anderson's influence continued to span the years following his demise, with much fresh ground being broken for critical estimates of his writings.

Concurrent with a new edition of his memoirs, it was felt that this was the appropriate time to bring back the homage and to include a selection of unpublished letters along with an essay, "THE MODERN WRITER" which had been issued in a limited edition in 1925.

Acknowledgements

To Eleanor Copenhaver Anderson for her whole hearted co-operation and support in granting permission to publish the letters selected for this edition.

To Maxwell Geismar for his encouragement and critical approval of the letters, and for his overall suggestions which I have tried to follow.

To my wife, Patricia, who, with love and understanding, helped me nurture an idea into reality.

Contents

Sherwood Anderson

by

THEODORE DREISER

ANDERSON, his life and his writings, epitomize for me
the pilgrimage of a poet and dreamer across this limited
stage called Life, whose reactions to the mystery of our
being and doings here (our will-less and so wholly auto-
matic responses to our environing forces) involved tenderness, love and beauty, delight in the strangeness of our
will-less reactions as well as pity, sympathy and love for all
things both great and small. Whenever I think of him I
think of that wondrous line out of "The Ancient Mariner"
—"He prayeth best who lovest best all things both great
and small." And so sometimes the things he wrote, as well as
the not too many things he said to me personally, had the
value of a poetic prayer for the happiness and the well being
of everything and everybody—as well as the well-outcoming
of everything guided as each thing plainly is by an enor-
mous wisdom—if seemingly not always imbued with mercy—
that none-the-less "passeth all understanding." He seemed to
me to accept in humbleness, as well as in and of necessity in
nature, Christ's dictums "The rain falleth on the just and
unjust." Also that we are to "Take no thought for your life,
what ye shall eat, or what ye shall drink: nor yet for your
body, what ye shall put on. Is not the life more than meat,
and the body than raiment?"

As I see him now there was something Biblical and pro-

1

phetic about him. Through all his days he appears to have been wandering here and there, looking, thinking, wondering. And the things he brought back from the fields of life! "Dark Laughter!" "Many Marriages!" "The Triumph of the Egg!" "Midwestern Chants!" "Winesburg!"—in which is that beautiful commentary on the strain of life on some temperaments called "Hands!" It is to me so truly beautiful, understanding and loving, and weeping, almost, for the suffering of others.

Well he is gone—wise, kind, affectionate, forgiving. And I wish he were not. To me, amidst all the strain of living and working, he was a comforting figure—never in any sense a slave to money, or that other seeming necessity to so many, show, or pretense. He was what he was and accepted himself in just that sense—"I am what I am."—"Take me or leave me for what I am to you." And I, like millions of others, I am sure, have taken him in just that sense. And other millions will, I feel, for the duration at least of our American literature.

The Man of Good Will

by

PAUL ROSENFELD

T
HE SCENE was the dining room of the Yale Club on a
spring day in 1917. Unusually at ease I was lingering over
lunch there with a broad-breasted kind of individual whose
wavy-haired, bullety-cheeked head and warm eyes, color of
iodine, by turns resembled those of an actor, a racetrack-sport,
a salesman, a Shelleyesque poet and half the population of
rural America. Weeks previous an entire Sunday had passed
unnoticed about me while, settled in an armchair captivated
by a sweeping new fiction "Windy McPherson's Son," I followed the fortunes of a hero who seemed intrinsically American as no other since Ragged Dick; indeed who seemingly was
Ragged Dick recovering from ambition as from an illness.
The balanced, flowing, satisfactory person now opposite me
was his author, Sherwood Anderson, the new Chicago writer.
A business trip had brought him to New York. We had met
at Waldo Frank's.

With an elbow on the cloth, one paw supporting his head
while the other occasionally and delicately plucked at some
grapes, my guest regaled me first with the tale of a female
Falstaff up in Michigan, then with a strong recent impression of Randolph Bourne, "the only man whose political talk
ever had interested him." I began telling him about another
brilliant young fellow, the pianist and composer Leo Orn-

3

stein; of his conception of universal sympathy as the possible
goal of existence. "Still, how are you going to feel in sympathy with policemen?" suddenly I asked, only half jocose,
glancing through the window across coppery rooves at the
emerging image of something beefy on a sidewalk, wooden
in its blue uniform, harboring readily inflammable brutality.
Hatred of those physical brethren, "New York's finest," was
one of the apparently irreducible remnants of a childhood.

Anderson leaned back, laughing, "Oh!" he drawled, "I
see them when they reach home at night. I see them taking
off their boots. Their feet hurt them." Involuntarily my
mind's eye met a small interior hovering apparently at a
short distance. It was the tenement kitchen of some police-
man in Chicago: what however filled the cubicle was no
battering-ram in blue but a coatless breathing male in the
suddenly significant act of slowly taking off a heavy shoe.
An air of authenticity enveloped the picture. The man's hand
began kneading the foot uncovered in its cotton sock. In-
stantly the interior turned into the unveiled privacy of all
policemen. Within the figure the nature of men in general
seemed rising to the surface. Promptly I recognized a human
being who got his bread with his brawn and paid for it like
everyone, with tired members. I smiled, aware of space curi-
ously before my chest; even more sharply aware of the presence of an amazing force in the peasant-like and highly
civilized being over the table, and its amazing mode of
operation.

Through the image of a familiar, well-nigh grotesque,
hitherto never clearly focussed detail, I quickly saw an idea
had been communicated to me; and at my own center, opposite it, antipathy and fear which hurt and shrunk me had
been dispelled, and a confidence in life permitted to emerge,
breathe, stretch itself. No quite similar experience ever had
befallen me. Behind the event, at its source I inferred a lifelong uninhibited approach to ordinary people and a phe-
nomenally keen faculty of observation; and glancing at my
guest, and catching the expression of what I took to be
merely personal benevolence, took personal benevolence to

be his essential attribute. For the moment my findings satisfied me. Still the experience lingered; expanded in my mind;
in the ensuing months convinced me that through the
Chicagoan's personality and his work a beautiful, extra-
ordinarily humanizing force was active in American life.
One could feel its presence in the new creative environment
America was fast becoming, as materially as the new qualities
of light growing plain along industrial avenues, the new
qualities of color which shone in brick factory walls. The
serialization of the exquisitely definite Winesburg stories
merely corroborated the conviction. Here were perfect
instances of the mode of communicating ideas, atmospheres,
destinies that singularly made one know one's fellow-country-
men, with almost grotesque images gleaned through observation of the commonplace life of the people in the small towns
and their curious quirks. The nature of the force at the root
of this imaginative, lyrical writing, it is true, remained
obscure to me. When people asked to know what it was I
saw in Anderson, I could, almost comically, only declare
"He's the man who told me about policemen!" and recount
the table talk. Nevertheless I had had direct, not to be forgotten contact with what in the final analysis is causing us
all in this issue of STORY to unite in commemorating his personality and work as one of the rare and representative
American expressions. I had been touched by the heroic
good will in Sherwood Anderson.

Deliberately I eschew the word Love. The essence was
less impassioned, breezier, more fraternal, more American
in fine, than that of Love. There was quiet benevolence in
it; a friendly inclination toward the human creature; a steady
open-eyed sympathy with him. It was the distillation of the
communal good will of the Middle West, whose finest
younger son Anderson was. The homesteaders, I take it,
craved neighbors; delighted in people. Anderson also delighted in men and women, drew them to him "like an open
fire." Participation in their existences warmed his spirits as
the bodies of the young girls warmed the blood of the old
David. His abomination was "the kind of young Lindbergh,

all machine—dreaming of seeing a mill that would employ
no people at all." But in Anderson the communal good will
had become disinterested, idealized. "I get nothing out of
anything in life except as it affects the lives of men and
women," he wrote in "Perhaps Women": it was that he was
looking for their fineness, sweetness, playfulness. The per-
sistence of touch and affection among them had become a
consummation. Thus with his interest, laughter, friendliness
he lavished perceptions and conciliatory interpretations on
life, inciting almost in every phrase to sympathy and understanding. Characteristically during the terrible winters of
'31 and '32 he found his role as the interpreter of class to
class, traveling through farmlands, mining towns, industrial
centers for the material of "Puzzled America"; talking with
men and women at work and out of it; acquiring new insight
into the fears, hopes, ideals of the bedrock people. Ironic,
satiric he could be at times; malicious, never. The unflagging
pompousness of Carl Sandburg of the "Lincoln" period, for
example, exasperated him: still he was ever ready all drolly
to make allowance for it. "I hold the Plains responsible," he
would say. "You know, they affected the Indians that way.
The Indians of the Plains used to give themselves names
like 'Sitting Bull' or 'Great Rain-In-The-Face.' I'm afraid
they've gotten old Carl, too." In later years he was most like
some tiny *sol* down in the mists of earth, sending his beams
horizontally through the atmosphere.

Humble, warm, the tone of his writings certainly refers
us to great good will in him. As certainly, the novel and
delightful pictures and symbols composing the more permanent portions of his free, natural, sometimes grotesquely
pathetic but oftentimes keenly, deeply, meaningful art refer
us to a clairvoyance which plausibly might have had its
origin in this disposition. Sparks cast up from the inner realm
of the American; with the look of truths that come swiftly,
half-poignantly, half-humorously winging in, these ideas,
perceptions, rhythmic states of mind point to swift fraternal
dilations of spirit and heart—which in combination with his
shrewdness placed him adventurously at the dynamic core

of his inarticulate compatriots, or caused him to find these undeciphered persons present to his soul and the forces of their discontinuous lives within his own. Significant too is the fact that one feels the visionary in Anderson one of those who provide the cement of free societies. By virtue of the "inner form" of his best prose, there was always an introduction—sincere and cordial—of essence to essence, interior to interior. With his objectification of elusive feelings; experiences of the power of intimacy; transmission of voices from solitary corners; reproductions of the moments of sensibility in which some wave of life briefly surges through the surface mechanization; above all, with his affable, confiding tone he created tolerance of and friendship for real selves.

Let them consider him passé at Harvard, of slighter consequence than Erskine Caldwell! Actually he is no less valuable to our culture than Walt Whitman! Like Whitman, he was rooted in the entire land, in its corn and people, sweetness and strength; his invention remains equally undetachable from this deep soil. No doubt Sherwood lacked the great poet's heroic strenuousness and cosmos-laden breath. At moments, as in "An Ohio Pagan," he began to have them; but his forte lay more in the shorter forms—in giving wings to "familiar" prose by relating it to the unutterable, the spasmodic movements of the American psyche in the Age of the Machine, the rapid intuitions and experience of the mind-and-body—and in instances his form and ideas were fumbled after. But it is impossible to overlook the masterly brio, grace and depth in the flow of the great stories of "The Triumph of the Egg" and "Horses and Men." Together with it he had unfailing rightness of feeling, selfhood like Whitman's, lyric depth, appreciation of life, the spirit of place. And where the man of Manhattan was an egoist, the Ohioan was a socialist in the words real meaning —and gave voice to the feeling of women as well as that of men.

Anderson naturally never talked about good will. It was too actual in him. Probably for the reason that it was so actual he gave up his business career—for "business" as has

been said, like the word for it, mainly is a matter of "I" and
"us." Possibly he himself was never more than semi-conscious
of his driving force. My own first knowledge of it arrived
circuitously enough. He had hunted me up of his own good
nature while I was a guest of the government's at a Sahara-
like army camp. After the war ended he lived for a while at
a rooming house in Chelsea—a perfect Winesburg it was:
one of the lodgers, an elderly bookkeeper, spent his evenings
building up sentimental landscapes on velvet with colored
threads of silk. There one afternoon I found the novelist
emitting visible sparks. It seemed an able but troublingly
ambitious colleague of ours had called on him and boasted
"Sherwood, you and I are the greatest short storytellers in
the United States!" Anderson had exclaimed, "Don't do that!
Don't you know that attitude is poison? No artist can afford
it!" Astoundingly the visitor had begun to cry, to protest that
he could not help what he did, the tendency to it being
innate in him, etc., etc. Anderson begged him to forget the
matter: they had gone for a walk together. Suddenly our
colleague recommended "Sherwood, some day you and I are
going to Paris, and down at the Gare St. Lazare waiting to
greet us will be Gide, Claudel, Jules Romains, Paul Valéry."
On the sidewalk Anderson had stopped short and turned on
him—one can see him doing it, the gesture was idiosyncratic
—with "There, you're at it again!" Opening childlike, still
not entirely comprehensive eyes, the man amiably had in-
quired "Oh, is *that* what you meant?" For my part I could
not help becoming aware of the clear talent's semi-instinctive
guardianship of an extroitive, impersonal direction of the
spirit, averse to selfishness and self-adulation: as the source
of his connection with universal life, and creativity; against
its internal no whit less than its external foes.

Then in May, 1921, Sherwood, Tennessee Mitchell, and
I crossed to Europe together; the experience deepened.
Among the passengers happened to be a pretentious little
politician, an ex-mayor of Chicago traveling to Paris to lay
a wreath, of course, on the Grave of the Unknown Soldier.
Most superior, at sundown every day His Honor took a con-

stitutional on deck, escorted in lieu of motorcycle police by
his lady wife. Once while the distinguished back and mangy
neck dwindled along the ship-rail Anderson, who ostensibly
was working at his rhapsodic "A New Testament," called
toward my chair in a chicken-voice, "Paul, do you think
Napoleon could have been a man like that?" I laughed, but
was shocked at Sherwood Anderson; thought that while
derogating the wish for distinction from one's fellows he
had expressed scepticism of the existence of superior abilities.
No hero-worshipper, I nonetheless honored the heroic; and I
suspected his ignorance. But I had been set, again circuitously, on the trail of Anderson's nobly-democratic values and
the underlying feeling. An incident in the Salle Rubens of
the Louvre, a few days after, proved it. . . . Sherwood was
overwrought on our first day in Paris. Crossing the court of
the Tuileries with him I fancied he'd gotten a cinder in his
eye, so vehemently was he rubbing the organ. He turned
aside, leaned an arm on the pedestal of a statue. It was tears.
"I never thought anything on earth could be so beautiful!"
he stammered; and glancing away, I took in the joyousness
of Paris in the flutter of countless flags on the long, silvery-
dark pavilions, the intimate blue-and-silver of the backdrop
low over the outstretched gardens; farther out, the man's
contrastive yearlong milieu . . . squalid, smoky Ohio, Cleveland, Akron, Youngstown, the paradise of the self-important;
and his inordinate sensitiveness to rightness and wrongness
in things.

A *consommation* at a café and the jubilant color the history
of Marie de' Medici restored the equilibrium. Before the
florid apotheosis of Henry of Navarre he stopped short and
chuckled "Henry! Henry!" He was remarking, it was plain,
on the astounding resemblance between the hero borne aloft
by Ruben's nymphs or throning on a rainbow and a Henry
who sold automobiles or insurance in Ohio. This time, nevertheless, I was too aware of Sherwood Anderson's wholeness
of nature, simplicity, fineness, to be fooled into thinking that
he intended to "debunk" my conception of the being we call
"the great man" and he insisted on calling "the Natural":

the individual of innate knowledge and unusual abilities. There was no tendency in him, I realized, to belittle greatness of deed, word, personality, even though he might suspect how many lights have owed their radiance to their chandeliers. If he ironized the vanity of wanting laurels, flambeaux, exaltations, ascensions, it was, I saw then and thenceforth, for two valid reasons. One was the unnecessary violence it had done to the face of the world and to the human society. The other was his vision of the slightness of the difference between the superior individual and the average one—the fruit of a sense of the inalienable, ineffable dignity and worth of life in any form. Life was the true wonder: the superior individual appeared little and lost in its far-spreading grandeur. A hand constituted more of a miracle than all works of art. Every Henry whether of Béarn or of a rooming-house "Winesburg" remained a unique, never-recurrent marvel. The content of the least conspicuous of human existences exceeded all which Shakespeare had expressed. True, the world was immediacably frustrate, melancholy, grotesque. Man was not God. But his drunken Dr. Parcival had spoken for Anderson when he told the lad "Everyone in the world is Christ."

Whence the road to the discovery of the attitude productive of this affirmation of life could not but prove a short one. All this will seem tantamount to claiming an angel's rank for Sherwood Anderson, when it might seem one could more reasonably have insisted that he was thoroughly an artist, revelling in his sense-impressions, the hissing of the corn, the humming of machinery; lost to himself in his objects; searching for their perfect expressions—an artist and a lord of life. Certainly, none will be more greatly surprised by the claim than he would himself have been. Still it would be insincerity to withhold that what one now hears him saying most clearly is the substance of a song, to the effect that glory belongs alone to God in the highest, and what belongs on earth is peace, good will to Men.

A Robin's Egg Renaissance*

by

SHERWOOD ANDERSON

I T WAS *a time of a kind of renaissance, in the arts, in litera-ture, a Robin's Egg Renaissance I have called it in my mind since. It fell out of the nest. It may be that we should all have stayed in Chicago . . . .*

There we would all have been chirping away and pecking at worms up and down Michigan Boulevard until this very day.

—S. A.

CHICAGO DAYS

Any American who has traveled much over the country comes finally to fix upon one city as his home city. He may have been born in a small town or on a farm but that particular city is his big town.

And that's what Chicago is to me. I went there, from a small Ohio town as a very young boy, saw my first play there, felt all of the terror and loneliness a small-town boy must feel pitched down alone in a great city. I was a laborer there, went from there to join the army, gradually made

---

*A fragment from Sherwood Anderson's forthcoming autobiography (*Har-court, Brace*).

friends, walked restlessly Chicago streets at night, became in love with Chicago women, wrote many of my best known stories there, hung over the old wooden bridges that formerly crossed the Chicago river, watching the gulls float over the river, got out of the ranks of labor and became a business man, began to scribble and was less and less good at my job, chucked the job and wandered away, came back to try again.

It was in Chicago that I first knew other writers and men interested in literature. It was in Chicago that the newspapers first both damned and praised my work.

And how many notable men known there, friends made. Justin Smith, Ferdinand Schevill, Robert Lovett, Burton Rascoe, Lloyd Lewis, Ben Hecht, Floyd Dell, Arthur Fickie, Harry Hansen, Carl Sandburg, Lewis Galantiere, Ernest Hemingway.

With these men and others I sat about in restaurants, talked of books, had the works of old writers brought to my attention, discussed new writers.

With Ben Hecht in particular I often went while he covered news stories. We quarreled and fought, made up, remained friends.

Other men, not to become literary figures made lifelong friends, the big Irishman George Dougherty, Roger Sergel, now at the head of The Dramatic Publishing Company. Talking also with these men of books and writers, drinking with them, sometimes spending most of the night walking and talking.

And there was the fascinating figure, Margaret Anderson. I knew her when she burst forth with her *Little Review*, wrote for her first number, wrote for the old *Dial* when it was published in Chicago, became a part of what was for a time called "the Chicago School" of writers.

How many men known, women known during the years there. They come flocking into my mind, men of the advertising office where I was for long years employed as copy writer, men infinitely patient with me and my idiosyncrasies.

And there was that rather glamorous fellow the Italian poet, Carnivali, who came from the east to help Harriet

Monroe on *Poetry Magazine,* he sometimes raging about my rooms at night.

And Bodenheim, with his corncob pipe and the broken arm he carried in a sling, although it was but an imagined break.

It was a time of a kind of renaissance, in the arts, in literature, a Robin's Egg Renaissance I have called it in my mind since. It fell out of the nest. It may be that we should all have stayed in Chicago.

So many of us began then, got our early impressions of life there, made friends there. Had we stayed in the home nest, in Chicago, when it all began for so many of us, the Robin's Egg might have hatched.

There we would all have been chirping away and pecking at worms up and down Michigan Boulevard until this very day.

SOUTH SIDE

It was an exciting time for me. I had come back to the city of Chicago after my adventure as a manufacturer. There was a great bag, full of manuscripts, with none of which I was satisfied. There were, if my memory does not now play me tricks, four long novels and any number of attempts at short stories, poems, essays. I had got a room in Fifty-seventh Street on Chicago's South Side and, after some hesitation, the advertising agency that had formerly employed me had taken me back.

"I do hope you'll go straight now."

This would have been Bayard Barton, who had now become president of the agency, talking to me. Bayard was too gentle a man to be really gruff.

"And what do you mean by going straight?"

The conversation would have taken place in his office.

"Well Bayard, you have certainly risen in the world." He had been a copy writer as I had been. We had got together in the same little hall of a room, writing of cough cures, fertilizers for farms, rouge for women's cheeks.

I had something on Bayard. Did he not formerly show me verses he had written?

And now he was lecturing me. It was an old story. From my own wife I had got just such lectures.

"It is about this scribbling of yours. You cannot have such divided interest. Either you are an advertising man or you are a writer."

"Yes, I know," I said. "You are about to speak now of my lack of education. Such men as myself, who are not college men, whose minds have not been disciplined, cannot become real writers. I have heard all of that, have heard it to weariness but I do not see that what I do after hours, when I am not employed here in this office, can matter to you."

He would have called my attention to my failure as a manufacturer.

"It was because your real interest was not in the business. And then besides I know well that, in coming back here, you are only coming because you are broke. You have no interest in advertising writing. In a month you will be swaggering before us, your tongue in your cheek."

"And writing down good copy for you," I said, laughing at him. For well I knew he would not turn me down. There was something between us, a kind of affection.

Had he not also once said to me that, when he had made his pile. . . . That was an old dream. No man or woman among us doing what he wanted to do. We were writing, dreaming, hoping.

"When I make my pile."

Among us writers the dream of writing for the popular magazines or the so-called "pulps," or if more lucky getting a script job in Hollywood. Big money to be made and put aside. Then some real work done.

It didn't seem to work out.

I sat looking at Bayard who was looking at me. There was a silence between us. We were both thinking of former days, when we had both been copy writers together, walks taken in the evening, talks we had.

"There is so much whoredom. I wonder if it is possible

to escape it. All of this spending our lives struggling to get a little ahead of the other fellow, make more money. It is a disease of our civilization."

Bayard, as copy writer had been sent down to write copy for Firestone tires, and Mr. Firestone had taken a fancy to him. He had a quality I did not have. He had felt a real obligation to Mr. Firestone and his huge organization. For the time the sale of more and more Firestone tires had become all important to him, and no doubt Mr. Firestone had appreciated what he had in the man Barton.

He had turned the account over to him, a huge one, and Bayard had been lifted up to his new position of power.

He could force his way up.

"Give me what I want or I will take the account somewhere else."

He had been made president of the company. Well, he was on his way to making his pile now. Poor man, he did not live long to enjoy it. You get into some such a position, in the world of business and where are you?

It is true some men can stand it. They go on and on accumulating and accumulating. To them at times the seemingly insane struggle is a kind of game at which they play.

But my friend Barton had other dreams. I saw the tired look in his eyes. Given the same opportunity he had had with Mr. Firestone I would, inevitably, have made some sarcastic remark. Then out I would have gone.

We sat looking at each other, sitting there in his luxurious office. We were both remembering vows we had taken to each other.

"I am going to keep something of myself out of this."

"It's true we advertising writers have to write a lot of bunk."

"The great thing is to know when we are writing bunk."

"We mustn't begin to believe in the bunk we write. We must keep honest minds."

"Oh, what the hell. You have chucked the attempt to be a manufacturer. You're broke and don't know where to turn. All right. Go to work. I'll give you a job for old time's sake."

Poor man, he was himself caught. He was a sensitive man, caught in the wheel. In two, three, four years he would be dead.

He arose from his desk. "Look here," he said. "You know how I got to where I am. I stole an account, a big one. I was proud and glad when I did it. . . . And now I have ahold of something and I can't let go. I don't know why but I can't. My pride is in some way involved. . . . So let me tell you something. If you ever have a chance to steal an account, take it away from me as I have taken the Firestone account from the others here, do not do as I did. Steal a little account, steal two or three little accounts. Do not get into the big time. Stay under the guns."

He laughed and turned away. Oddly enough I did later steal two or three small accounts from him and when I did it he laughed again.

There wasn't however, on each occasion, much joy in his laughter. He was no longer the old Bayard Barton with whom, when we were both younger, I had walked and talked on many a summer evening while we told each other of our dreams.

I had taken rooms in Fifty-seventh Street and there I was, back in the old grind. However I did have my evenings and there were the week ends. I began again at my stories, the piles of manuscript, all I had written in the room at the top of the house in the Ohio town where for five years I had been struggling to be what nature did not intend me to be—a man of business.

They were there before me, the attempt at short stories, the long novels, the piles of verses, piled high on a long table I had bought at a second-hand store.

And what peace and quiet in the room. I wonder now how much I thought then of the matter of publication, of becoming a real author. It seems to me that I did not take all that too seriously. For years I had been going about, observing, making notes in my mind. My own life, the living of my own life, had seemed most unsatisfactory to me.

In the Ohio town I had been for a time seemingly on the
road to success.

And then had come a sudden sickening. I had been married. I had children. I had been unfaithful to my wife.
Always I had been doing things that shocked and hurt some
inner part of me but I kept on doing them. I had begun
drinking and, for a time, had been on the way to becoming
a drunkard. I left my home town and went to Cleveland.
I went from saloon to saloon, picking up men companions.
I became drunk with them, went with them to houses of
prostitution.

There had been one tall, rather handsome prostitute who
had taken a fancy to me.

"You be my man," she said.

I had been sitting about in the parlor of such houses with
companions picked up. Men were drinking with the women
of the place. Now and then one of them disappeared up a
stairway with one of the women.

So it had come to that, the relationship between men and
women of which I had dreamed such dreams in my boyhood.
Come to that.

"And why am I here?"

I kept asking myself that question. I kept drinking. I became drunk and fell off the chair in which I had been sitting.

I had spent the night in that place. The tall woman had
taken care of me. I awoke there in the morning.

I was on a couch, in a little alcove off what was called the
parlor of the house and presently there was that tall woman
sitting beside me. We began to talk.

It was a strange conversation. When I had become drunken
on the night before, some of the other women of the place,
along with the men with whom I had come there, had
wanted to undress me. The idea had been to expose me to
the view of all who came into the place. They had planned
to paint my body, decorate certain very private parts of my
body, make a kind of vulgar spectacle of me, but the tall
woman had stopped it. She told me of that. She had, she

said, a brother at home, who was much like me.

"Did you come here to get a woman?" she asked and I told her that I had not come with that in mind.

I had come to that place, as I got drunk, in an effort to escape from myself.

"There is something about myself I do not like."

There is, I realize, a danger of sentimentalizing all this. Men are always doing that in regard to prostitutes. All I can be sure of is that, on that morning, I had left that place, filled with shame, my eyes taking in the street as I emerged from the door and hurried away. The shame doubled when, on a street nearby I passed some children playing on the sidewalk. Later, on two or three occasions I did see the tall prostitute again. In a kind of spirit of defiance I phoned to her. I invited her to dine with me at one of the big Cleveland hotels, took her on a certain fall afternoon to the trotting meeting, walked in streets with her, was seen in her presence by men from my town where I was a respectable manufacturer.

And all of this out of a spirit of defiance, wanting in some way to defy the respectable money-making, scheming money-grasping life of which I had been part.

"And do you want to be my man?" The tall woman was puzzled. "It would be a little like sleeping with my own brother. You and he look so alike."

There was of course her own story told to me. Whether it was a true story or not I cannot say. It was all connected with the brother whom it seemed I resembled. He did not know what she was doing. He was, she declared, a student in a college in the West, the University of the State of Wisconsin.

"We are Italians," she said. She was getting her brother started in life. He was to have no idea of what she had been doing. When she had seen him through college, had got him established, she would no longer be a prostitute.

"More than one woman who has been a whore has afterward turned out to be a good wife to some man," she said.

"Do you want to be my man, my special man? Well I do

not want you to be. It would be too much like being with my own brother."

Such happenings in my life. Obviously that tall woman wanting something outside the life she was living, kind of grasping at a friendship. Or so it had seemed to me.

Myself struggling to get at something outside the life of buying and selling, finding it in the writing.

So there it was, more and more of it accumulating on my desk, great piles of it.

One day my older brother Karl, an established painter, came to the city. He was having an exhibition of his paint-ings and while he was in the city came to stay with me in my rooms.

"What is this? So you are writing now." He picked up one of the novels I had written, took it away with him. He took me into a new world. It began with his visit.

He had taken one of my novels, the one later published under the title of "Windy McPherson's Son," to Mr. Floyd Dell with whom he had become acquainted and who was then the editor of the special Friday book section of the Chicago *Post.* It was a position that had been held by Mr. Francis Hackett and Dell had been his assistant. But Hack-ett had gone off to New York, to become one of the editors of the newly established *New Republic,* and Dell had be-come the literary editor of the *Post,* with Lucian Cary as his assistant.

So there was Dell reading my novel and presently, in the columns of the Friday *Post,* writing of me.

I was, it seemed, the great unknown.

Why, how exciting! There I was, as Dell was saying in print, in a newspaper read as I presumed by thousands, an unknown man (I do not now remember whether or not he mentioned my name) doing, in obscurity, this wonderful thing.

And with what eagerness I read. If he had not printed my name, at least he had given an outline of my novel. There could be no mistake.

"It's me. It's me."

I would have pranced excitedly up and down in my room. "I must know this man."

It seemed to me that I had, of a sudden been chosen, elected as it were, given a kind of passport into some strange new and exclusive world.

It was true that I had already published a story. It had appeared in *Harper's Magazine* and had been called "The Rabbit Pen," but I had not taken the story very seriously, had not been much excited by its publication.

The story, in fact had been written in answer to a kind of challenge. An old friend, Miss Trilena White, a schoolteacher with whom I had become acquainted when I was, for a brief time, a student at Wittenberg College at Springfield, Ohio, had come to visit at my house and there had been much talk of William Dean Howells, a man she much admired.

At the time Howells was editing what was called "The Easy Chair" section of *Harper's*.

I had made some sharp criticism of Howells and my friend had challenged me.

"They are all of them, Howells, Twain, Hawthorne, too much afraid," I had declared. "In all their writing there is too much of life left out."

There was, for example, the matter of sex. My own experience in living had already taught me that sex was a tremendous force in life. It twisted people, beat upon them, often distracted and destroyed their lives.

"It must be that these men know what an influence it is on lives but they are afraid of it. Twain, for example, had written and published privately, or at least it had been published, I had seen it, a thing he called *Conversations in the Court of Queen Elizabeth*."

But what about conversation in everyday American life, in saloons, in the backs of stores, in factories, workshops and streets?

"And I daresay often enough among American women too? Why hesitate to put down whatever is in men and women's lives, making the picture whole? I tell you that some day, soon now, men will come. . . ."

My criticism of Howells and others had a little offended my friend.

"Why I myself can write a story that *Harper's* will print."

I had made the boast. The story I wrote and that was published was not the kind of story I was already feeling my way toward. Its publication had merely been a sort of triumph over my friend.

But here I was now in Chicago and here was Dell writing in a newspaper of an unpublished novel of mine. I had got a letter from Marjorie Curry, Floyd Dell's wife, asking me to come.

I went, filled with excitement. Now I was to go into a new world, men and women whose interests would be my interest, the curious feeling of loneliness and uncertainty broken up. I thought of the nights when I could not work, the hours spent walking the city streets, great projects forming in my mind, these coming to nothing.

I went to the address, at the corner of Fifty-seventh and Stony Island Avenue and found there a row of low, one-story buildings. The buildings had been, I was later told, hurriedly thrown up at the time of the Chicago World's Fair. There had been stores there but now they had become the homes of men and women of Chicago's intellectual and artistic set. On that first night I walked back and forth before the store fronts. Curtains had been put up and now they were drawn and behind the curtains in the rooms I could hear voices. Shouts of laughter went up. A voice began to sing.

I had my hand on the doorknob of the Dell house (it was indeed a single large room that had once been a retail store; a partition had been thrown up, at the back and a kind of kitchenette made), but I lost courage.

"Why these must be indeed quite wonderful people but would they really receive me?"

How many times had I been told that, by spending my time scribbling away at stories I was but wasting my time and energy. That, it had been pointed out to me, was a field for educated men, and I was not educated. I spelled badly.

It was a curse that was to cling to me all my life. I knew nothing of punctuation; to save my life could not have *phrased* a sentence. It was true that I had read eagerly, since childhood, but for most of my life I had associated with workingmen; had been, for a time, a hanger-on of race horse men. To associate with advertising writers was one thing. But to be in the actual company of men who had perhaps actually written books that had been published, who wrote learnedly of books in newspapers and magazines was another.

All of this is I know a little absurd, but there I was. I was at the door of Dell's little one-room house and I went away. I went to walk in Jackson Park.

"This is absurd. You are being cowardly. They may indeed be kind to you. They may help you," I told myself. I remembered how Dell had written of my own unpublished book and returned again to the door. But again I left without daring to enter.

Then on a day perhaps a week later, I did enter. I had come home early from the office and went to stand in the park until I saw little Marjorie Curry .enter alone.

A new life began for me. As had been the case with me time and time again, Marjorie Curry, like other women I have known, was infinitely kind to me. At once she made me feel at home.

"Come," she said at once, "we will go for a walk in the park."

We did walk and she told me of her friends. It was through Marjorie that I met Ben Hecht, Arthur Fickie, her husband Floyd Dell, who became for a time a kind of literary father to me. Their marriage was at the time breaking up, as my own had broken up, and this fact may have drawn me closer to Marjorie. In her company I saw the poet Eunice Tietjens. Lucian Cary came to her house. I went with her and Ben Hecht to a town down state where Ben, then a star reporter on the *Daily News,* was covering a murder trial and a hanging. Summer came and we went off, often a great crowd of us to some little town on the lake. . . . It was during that summer that I met Carl Sandburg; Michael Carmichael

Carr, that infinitely charming man with the red beard and
the endless flow of talk, came from the University of Missouri; Alexander Kuhn, a Russian Jew, short and squat of
frame, came to tell us stories of life in Russia, of the perse-
cution of the Jews there, of life in little Russian villages;
Ernestine Evans, that strange world traveler, later always
turning up in some unexpected place, in Europe or the Far
East (I was to see her later in several European cities but was
to have occasional notes from her from all over the world),
was then newly graduated from the University of Chicago
and had taken, for living quarters, one of the vacant store
rooms near Marjorie. She brought Robert Lovett to her
rooms. Lewellyn Jones came. Through Ben Hecht I met
Justin Smith of the *News*; Burton Rascoe, then doing books
for the *Tribune*; and Lewis Galantiere who was to become
a lifelong friend.

It was a time of something blossoming in Chicago and the
Middle West. At the very moment, Edgar Lee Masters must
have been writing his "Spoon River Anthology" in Springfield; down the state Vachel Lindsay was shouting forth his
stirring verses; Dreiser, from Terre Haute in Indiana, had
written and published his "Sister Carrie"; and Margaret
Anderson, still working as editor of some church paper, was
soon to break loose and start her *Little Review*.

It was a time of excitement, something seemingly new and
fresh in the air we breathed, and there was little Marjorie,
who had rather taken me under her wing, who was then
employed as a reporter on the *Daily News* and who knew
so well all of these to me seemingly so wonderful people.

And what cannot such a woman do for such a man as I
was then! I have spoken a good deal here of my fears but
I do not believe that my fears were based on lack of faith
in my own talent. I was then as I have always been, not a
proud but an infinitely vain man. At bottom I was an egoist,
as Ben Hecht once said of me, so much the egoist that nothing ever really touched the central core of my egoism.

"Why I can write as well as any man alive. I have not
come to it yet but I will come to it," I was always secretly

saying to myself. Among the men at all interested in books
and writing I had known, until that summer, O. Henry had
been time and time again pointed out to me as the great
American storyteller. But I did not think he was great. "He
had learned too many tricks," I thought. I thought that Mark
Twain, in his "Huckleberry Finn," and Melville, in his
"Moby Dick," had been our great tale tellers. I was myself
a man outside the schools. At the time, and not until years
later did I come to Chekhov or to Turgenev and his "Annals
of a Sportsman," but I had found the delightful and swaggering George Borrow.

I was, I knew, in a curious position. Although I had been
a passionate reader, my reading had never had any fixed
direction. There were whole continents of literature that I
had never visited. My own vocabulary was small. I had no
Latin, no Greek, no French. When I wanted to arrive at
anything like delicate shades of meaning in my writing, I
had to do it with my own very limited vocabulary.

And even my reading had not much increased my vocabulary. Oh, how many words I knew in books that I could not
pronounce!

But should I use in my writing words that were not a part
of my own everyday speech, of my own everyday thought?

I did not think so.

"No," I had long been telling myself, "you will have to
stay where you have put yourself." There was the language
of the streets, of American towns and cities, the language of
the factories and warehouses where I had worked, of laborers'
rooming houses, the saloons, the farms.

"It is my own language, limited as it is. I will have to learn
to work with it." There was a kind of poetry I was seeking
in my prose, word to be laid against word in just a certain
way, a kind of word color, a march of words and sentences,
the color to be squeezed out of simple words, simple sentence
construction. Just how much of all of this had been thought
out, as I have spoken of it here, I do not now know. What
I do know is the fact of the limitations I had to face.

And then, too, there was something else. I felt then, as I
am sure most of the men of the time did feel, that writing,

the telling of tales, had got too far away from life as we men
of the time were living our lives and what was so wonderful
to me, in the new associates I had found, was a certain boldness of speech.

We were in fact wallowing in boldness. At the time Freud
had just been discovered and all the young intellectuals were
busy analyzing each other and everyone they met. Floyd
Dell was hot at it. We had gathered 'in the evening in one
of the rooms. Well, I hadn't read Freud, in fact never did
read him and was rather ashamed of my ignorance. Floyd
walked up and down before us. He was at that time wearing
a stock and looked, I thought, like pictures I had seen of
Poe. When he was on the subject of literature he talked,
I thought, brilliantly. I had never before heard such talk.
How it flowed from him! What vast fields of literature he
covered! He became excited. He shouted. The intense little
figure became more and more erect.

And now he had begun psyching us. Not Floyd alone but
others in the group did it. They psyched me. They psyched
men passing the street. It was a time when it was well for a
man to be somewhat guarded in the remarks he made, what
he did with his hands. On a certain evening, when there
were several of us gathered together in a room, in an unfortunate moment I brought up the subject of homosexuality.
I was puzzled. Some years before, when I was newly come
to Chicago, when I was employed as a laborer in a North
Side warehouse, I had for the first time seen homosexuality
that was unashamed.

It had happened that, in that place, I worked a part of the
time on an unloading platform at the warehouse door. The
warehouse was on a street on the very North Side and in a
house further down the street several men lived together.

I was a small-town young man newly come to the great
city. At home, in our town there had been, to be sure, certain
men and boys who were somewhat feminine as there were
women and girls who seemed somewhat on the male side.

We others had called such boys "sissies." They were no
good at baseball, or at football. (I imagine that it must have
been somewhat the so-called Rugby sort. We did not carry

the ball. We kicked it up and down the field, often enough kicking one another rather than the ball.) They walked with mincing steps, often outdid us all in the classes, spoke with soft feminine vocies.

But these others, these of the city on the street of the warehouse, came by our platform sometimes in groups. They had painted cheeks and lips.

The others, the workmen and truckmen on the platform with me, shouted at them. "Oh, you Mabel!" "Why, if there isn't sweet little Susan."

The men passing who were so much like women, giggled at us.

There was a tall German who worked beside me. He began to swear. "If one of them made a pass at me I'd knock his goddam block off," he declared.

Once when I was alone on the platform (it was late fall and darkness had come), one of them stopped and spoke to me. He approached and whispered to me, "Don't you want to come and see me some night?"

I didn't answer, was a little shocked and even frightened.

"I have had my eye on you. You do not shout insults at us as the others do. You know where I live. Do come some night. There is so much I could teach you." He went off along the street, turning to throw a kiss at me and I stood dumbly staring at him.

What did it all mean? I felt a strange unhealth within myself. I was not angry and am quite sure that when this happened I felt even a kind of pity. There was a kind of door opened, as though I looked down through the door into a kind of dark pit, a place of monstrous shapes, a world of strange unhealth.

It is difficult now, as I write after the years, to remember just all I did feel on that occasion when first I came face to face with a fact in many other human lives. In the years since, several such men have come to me and have talked to me of their terrible problem, some few stories of my own, the story "Hands" in the volume "Winesburg" and the story I called "The Man Who Became a Woman" in the other volume "Horses and Men," having led them to think I could sympathize with them in their fight. But at the time, during the summer when I first found comrades in the little places in Fifty-seventh Street in Chicago, I was, on the whole, only puzzled.

So I asked the question, "What makes men like that?"

I went further. Perhaps I expressed a kind of fear of something in life I couldn't understand. And the fear in me was pounced upon.

Why, I was myself unconsciously one of them. The thing was in me too and the fear I had expressed was a sure sign of its presence. On another occasion when I had been walking in the park on a Sunday afternoon with one of my new acquaintances, we sat on a bench and as we talked of books and life I leaned over and picking up a twig from the path before us began to break it between my fingers and "Oh!" he exclaimed.

It seemed he had found me out. I was breaking the twig between my fingers and obviously, he explained to me, the twig was a phallic symbol. I was wanting to destroy the phallic in myself. I had secretly a desire to be a woman.

But it was not all like that. What nights we had, what excursions at the week ends! There was in us, I am sure, something of the fervor that must have taken hold of those earlier Americans who had attempted to found communistic communities. We were, in our own minds, a little band of soldiers who were going to free life (first of all, to be sure, our own lives) from certain bonds.

It wasn't exactly free love we wanted. I doubt that there was with us any more giving way to the simple urge of sex than among the advertising and business men among whom I worked for certain hours each day. Indeed sex was to be given a new dignity. And as for marriage, well it was obvious that on all sides of us there were men and women living the lives of married men and women without love, without tenderness.

I think we wanted to reveal something. Later my own observation of life in small Middle Western towns, as boy and young man, was to lead to the writing of my "Wines-burg, Ohio" and it has been said of the Winesburg stories that they did give storytelling among us a new turn.

We had been brought up on English literature, sifted down to us through New England; on walls of houses all over America pictures of Longfellow, Whittier, Emerson. The New Englanders had lived in a cold stony land. There were the little fields, surrounded by the stone walls. Through a large part of the year the skies were cold and forbidding overhead.

Puritans, oh? Well, I daresay they were no more pure than we of the Middle West. They were in Ohio, Indiana, Illinois, Southern Michigan, Iowa. Their blood had been mixed with that of those pushing up from the South, with those who had pushed down through Pennsylvania into the valley of Virginia and over the mountains, and through Cumberland Gap, into Kentucky and on into the Middle Western states bordering on the Ohio river.

These joined also by men of North Carolina, Scotch-Irish, many of them. They would have come also seeking the warm deep soil of the Middle Western states.

There was an empire there, Chicago its capital, to become the bread basket of the nation. My own father would have come up that way, from the North Carolina country. By his own story, or rather by one of his stories, he would have been of Scotch-Irish blood. In another book of my own, "A Story-Teller's Story," I have told of how he, when he was in the company of Germans, became a German, when with Italians an Italian, when with the Irish an Irishman.

And, I dare say, the North Carolina soil was rather thin and sandy too; a place of small farms, a few slaves, more poverty. My friend Paul Green, one of the great storytellers I have known, has told me enough rare, often Rabelasian tales of the North Carolinians.

Anyway there we were, intellectually dominated by New England. We wanted to escape from it. If European litera-ture had not much come into our Middle West, the Europeans had come. We had got the Irish, the Germans, the Swedes, Danes and Norwegians. There was a new race being made.

And we had seen, in the towns and villages of our Middle West, a kind of life going on that was reflected by our story-tellers. We had all read our "Huckleberry Finn," that amazingly beautiful book; something of the whole vast valley of the Mississippi in it, but it was after all a tale of childhood.

But what about the real life on the Mississippi, on the river boats, in Natchez under the hill, in certain districts of St. Louis and New Orleans? What stories really told in the pilot houses of river boats. Abe Lincoln, telling his stories in little taverns in Illinois, stories told in the back rooms of saloons in the towns in which we had lived; our own experience of thwarted lives, often sex bottled up as it were in women, twisted lives in New England, to become so feminine a world, so many of the men striking out into the richer Middle West, leaving their women behind.

Howells shushing Twain, so many of the stronger words of our everyday speech absolutely barred in our writing.

I do not think that any of us, at that time, wanted to over-play sex. We wanted in our stories and novels to bring it back into its real relation to the life we lived and saw others living.

I remembered an experience of my own. I had for a time, when I was newly come to the city—this when I was still working as a laborer—been at a certain home. They were people to whom I had been given a note of introduction and I went to call.

There were a great many books in that house, and I was hungry for books. Seeing there a volume of Walt Whitman I borrowed it, but when I got it home to my own room, in a workingman's rooming house, I found certain pages torn from the book.

I was curious. I managed to get ahold of an unmutilated volume and discovered the reason. Old Walt had simply expressed in certain verses, his healthy animalism and they couldn't take it. The idea being that it would be terribly corrupting to read, in the printed pages of a book what was so much in all our minds.

Or another experience, this out of my own life in a country town, before I came to the city.

I had gone to the house of a certain girl at night, on a Sunday night. I had, in fact, met with her as she emerged from church.

We had walked about. It was a summer evening and we were both young. We began to kiss.

We went to her house and sat on a porch at the back of the house. It was dark there.

And now she was lying on the floor of the porch. "I am sleepy," she said. She pretended to go to sleep. "Take me if you please. Do take me. Do it while I sleep. I must pretend to you that I do not know what is going on."

It ended so and later she could pretend to me and even perhaps to herself, that she did not know what had happened, that it had happened in her sleep.

All of this in relation to something now in my own life that I found among new people in the little converted retail store room at Fifty-seventh and Stony Island Avenue in Chicago—Floyd Dell, Arthur Fickie, Lawrence Langner—coming now and then from New York, to blow us out, give us perhaps a feast with drinks, Ben Hecht, Alexander Kuhn, occasional young professors from the University, talk and more talk.

A kind of healthy new frankness in the talk between men and women, at least an admission that we were all at times torn and harried by the same lusts.

Our own lusts a little faced. It meant everything to me. And then excursions at the week end, to the country, often to the low country, the quite wild South of Chicago.

Ben Hecht, having just read Flaubert, walking up and down declaiming. Ben then, as he remained, full of strange oaths, adjectives falling over adjectives. Mike Carr, with his little red beard and light-filling red bathing trunks (for hours he would recite verses). Alexander Kuhn, telling tales of life

in Russian villages. Myself, for the first time hearing of
Russian writers—Tolstoy, Dostoeveski, Chekhov, Turgenev
—a new world of writers to be opened up to me later.

Was I not later to be called, by one of our American critics,
"The Phallic Chekhov"?

I am trying to give here an impression of what was to me
a gay happy time, the gayest and happiest I have ever known;
a feeling of brotherhood and sisterhood with men and women
whose interests were my own. As yet I had not begun to face
what every practitioner of any art must face, the terrible
times of depression, of bitter dissatisfaction with the work
done; often the difficulty of making a living at your chosen
work, the facing of the petty jealousies that pop up among
fellow craftsmen, the temptation, always present to try to
get into the big money by attempting to "give them what you
think they want"; the times when the ink will not flow, when
you have worked, perhaps for weeks and months on some
project only to have to face the fact, on some sad morning,
that it is all N.G.; that what you have attempted hasn't come
off and must be thrown away.

All of this still ahead of me during that summer in Fifty-
seventh Street with my newly found fellows.

And then the women. How we do need them! There were
two Marjories, Marjorie Curry, who had been Floyd Dell's
wife, and Marjory Jones. It is to such women that a man
takes his first work.

"Now you tell me frankly what you think."

To be sure a man doesn't mean that. What he wants is
praise, to be reassured and it is this that women understand.
For often enough, for the young worker, it is only praise
that helps.

"Yes. You have real talent. Do not be afraid."

Such a woman will often remember for years some sentence you have written . . . and how it stirs and flatters a man
to have such a sentence remembered and repeated. It is a
special gift some women have, due perhaps to a lack of the
competitive feeling in them, they wanting to make you happy
and being not too scruplous about it. Thank Heaven for that.

For the road is very long. To accomplish anything in any of the arts worth remembering through a winter day is so difficult.

So there was that summer, to be always remembered; the days got through in the advertising place and then the summer evenings, the walks in the park, the gatherings in one of the little rooms; Arthur Fickie, then a young lawyer at Davenport, Iowa, but already itching to throw all of that over and devote himself to poetry, coming to town to give us a blowout. Wine, whiskey and beer brought in. Some sang. Hecht, trying out a play in a tiny theatre arranged in one of the rooms. Langner, the New York patent attorney interested in the theatre, come to Chicago perhaps on business, but devoting his evenings to us.

Then the week ends at some little town on the lake shore, six or eight of us men and women sleeping perhaps, or at least trying to sleep, under one blanket by a low fire built on the shore of the lake; even perhaps going off in the darkness to some secluded spot to bathe, all of us in the nude, it all quite innocent enough but such a wonderful feeling in us of leading a new, free, bold life, defying what seemed to us the terribly stodgy life out of which we had all come. And then perhaps a walk during the evening alone with one of the women.

For me it would have been with little Marjorie Curry, her hand on my arm. I would have given her an attempt at a story, to read.

"Do not be afraid, Sherwood. You have real talent. You will do it. You will do it."

Oh wonderful words!

Songs being sung by a fire on the beach at night.

"Have you read Stephen Crane's 'Maggie, A Girl of the Streets'?" Men and women, far more widely read than I was, talking and talking. Poems recited. Myself taking notes.

"I'll read that, I'll get it tomorrow."

It was all, I daresay, in the great dreams we had, the vows of comradeship taken, a little childish, an interlude for most of us faced with the difficulty of what we wanted to do.

Some of us were to fail dismally enough; all of us have to go through years of disappointment to accomplish little enough. But for us that summer was a gay time; for me, at least, a happy time.

Comradeship. How life and the living of lives here in America tears us apart.

BEN AND BURTON

When we were all in Chicago—Ben Hecht, Burton Rascoe, Lewis Galantiere, Justin Smith, Carl Sandburg, Harry Hansen and a half dozen others—we used to dine often at a place called Slagel's on Fifth Avenue. Later I believe the name of the street was changed. It became Wells Street. The *Daily News* was in a ramshackle old building over there under the elevated railroad.

We all dined around a big table and indulged in literary talk. At that time Henry Mencken was our great hero. We all read the old *Smart Set* and later Mencken and Nathan's *Mercury*. Many of us had got letters from Mencken. He was the great letter writer. At that time he must have been in correspondence with all of the young writers in the country. It must have paid the *Mercury* well. A man was in great luck who got more than twenty-five dollars for a story from that point.

Still we got the letters and the letters made us proud. "Well, I had a letter from Henry Mencken today."

You said it offhand, but in your heart you felt that it was like being knighted by a king.

You knew damn well the others felt the same. Henry made a great mistake. He should have, at just that time, made were, for the time, loaded up with Cabell's books. a grand tour—as Gertrude Stein did later, picking, as Gertrude did, just the right moment. In Chicago we would have delivered the town to him.

A few years before Francis Hackett and Floyd Dell had been the literary bandmasters in Chicago but they had both departed for New York, Hackett to the *New Republic* and

Floyd to the old *Masses*. Floyd published a novel that Hackett reviewed and the review was a masterpiece. He took Floyd's skin off inch by inch. It was the best job of literary skinning I ever read.

They were both however now gone from Chicago and Burton Rascoe, on the *Tribune*, and Ben Hecht, on the *Daily News*, were doing books for the town.

We were all at lunch and an agreement was made. I think it must have been Ben Hecht who proposed it.

"Look here, Burton, we'll take up some writer. You go big for him and I'll go against him. We'll keep it up. You blow your horn and I'll put on the Bronx Cheer."

I think something of that sort must have been said. At any rate the agreement was made and, as usual, Ben had got himself into an advantageous position.

Abuse was meat and drink to him. He loved it. He was a genius at it. Later, I am told he used the talent with wonderful effect on the movie magnates of Hollywood. I am told that the more he abused them the more they paid him. He could do it with a smile on his face.

The point is that it was all fun to Ben, in reality a very sweet man, full of kindnesses. But it was temporarily poison to Burton.

For Burton was then, as he always was, a highly nervous, sensitive man. He was easily hurt.

The two men had decided upon James Branch Cabell as the man to be praised and abused. They began and I have no doubt that Burton, although Ben had proposed the plan, had proposed the man. He was sincere in his admiration for Cabell while Ben was out to be vehemently insincere.

It began; it was carried on for weeks. Columns in the newspapers were filled with it and the Chicago bookstores

For the bookdealers it didn't, I was told, turn out so well. Too many people, induced to buy by all the clamor being raised, brought the books back.

They said they didn't understand the books.

They were too sophisticated, they said.

In Chicago at that time, among us who were literarily

inclined, there was a great passion to be sophisticated but our rank was small in numbers. Ben and Burton were over-selling the possible Cabell market.

It had all begun by the praise and abuse of Cabell but presently it became more personal. Ben began to call his opponent the sophomoric Rascoe and Rascoe attempted to meet Ben halfway in the matter of personal abuse.

It was for him a hopeless struggle, although, naturally, he had made of Cabell a lifelong friend and you can understand that. Cabell later dedicated a book to Burton. Under the circumstances I would have done the same.

It had all been begun as a stunt but it had grown serious. Now Ben and Burton, when they met, did not speak. Ben grinned and Burton frowned. Two men who had been and later were to become again real friends were, for the time, bitter enemies.

I decided to give a dinner and invited ten or twelve men. I invited Ben without telling Burton and when I invited Burton did not tell him that Ben was coming.

The dinner came off and we all sat at a long table. Burton and Ben opposite each other and Ben was in fine feather. He talked. He made insidious remarks, for the most part directed at Cabell. He did not look at Burton but kept addressing his remarks to the others at the table.

Burton kept hopping up and down in his chair. He could not eat. He kept opening and closing his mouth. He stuttered. There was a bottle of whiskey on the table and he kept filling his glass. I am quite sure that at the moment he was so excited that he did not realize that he was not drinking water.

And then at last he spoke. Burton, as all his friends know, always was, to the last inch, a literary man. He pointed a trembling finger at Ben.

"You talk," he shouted. "You think you know something about life, about literature. But what do you know of life? You tell me. You answer me. What do you know of life?"

Burton turned from Ben to the rest of us. He spoke of Ben with infinite scorn.

"You look at him. What does he know of life?"

Then the really tremendous statement that set the table roaring and in the end patched up the broken friendship came from Burton's lips. "This Ben Hecht," he said. "He knows nothing of real life. Why the man has never had but one mistress and she was a charwoman."

It was the final literary thrust. It broke something. It was all of England's literature come to our modest dinner table. When he had said it even Burton had to laugh. It patched everything up; made Burton and Ben what they had been before the great Cabell was begun—again warm and intimate friends.

RETROSPECT: JAN. 1940

On taking Eleanor to the room where I wrote Winesburg

It is the most difficult moment of all to write of. You are in a room. The particular room in which I sat was in an old house, old as Chicago houses go.

Once it had been the house of some fashionable family. The family had moved into some other, some newly fashionable section of the city. There had been one of those sudden shifts of the rich and fashionable, from one section of the city to another, so characteristic of our American cities. There had been a bathroom on the third floor of the house but now, that whole section of the city having fallen into a place of cheap rooming houses, thin partitions had been put up. There were many little rooms separated by thin partitions and they were all occupied.

The occupants were all young. They were young musicians, painters, young women who aspired to be actors. I have always wanted to write of the people of that house. They were, for the time, so close to me.

I was no longer young. I was the oldest in that house. At the time the room in which I lived seemed large and later, in my thoughts, it kept growing larger.

I often described it to my wife.

"There was a great desk," I said, "as long as this room in which we now stand." I described for her my bed, the shelves built into the wall. I have always, when at work, loved to walk up and down. I am sure I gave her the impression of myself striding up and down a long room, grown in my imagination into something like a great hall; the council room of a king.

And then once, years after I had lived there, I made the mistake of taking her to the house.

It was still a cheap rooming house. We drove up in a cab.

Why how shabby it had grown. There were dirty, torn lace curtains at the windows, and, as we went into the little hallway on the ground floor, the door being open, we came upon a young couple engaged in a quarrel. They stood facing us, paying no attention to our entrance. The woman was young. Her hair was in disorder and a cigarette burned between her fingers.

The quarrel was over money. He was accusing her of taking money from his pockets.

"Liar. Liar," she screamed at him.

She ran suddenly up a flight of stairs, the man following and we heard a door slam.

The landlady appeared. She was a short, fat woman of fifty clad in a torn dirty dress.

I wanted to run away. I didn't.

"We are looking for a room," I said and followed her silently up first one and then another flight of stairs. In a room on the second floor, behind a closed door there was the sound of a woman crying.

That would be the woman we just saw, quarreling with her man down below, I thought.

We had got to the door of the room. How heavy I felt. My feet were heavy.

"This room is unoccupied," the landlady said. Her hand was on the doorknob.

"Don't," I wanted to scream. "Don't open that door. Leave me my dream of the room, what it was."

The door opened.

Why what a shabby little hole. It was all tawdry, the room so small, the wall paper so dirty.

"We will go there. If the room is unoccupied we will spend a day, a week there." I had dreamed of sitting with her at the window that looked down toward the Chicago Loop in the evening, as the day faded, as the lights flashed on in the great buildings of the Loop.

People passing along the street below the window, passing under the street light at a nearby corner—shabbily dressed old men, smartly dressed young women. The house had stood just at the edge of the once fashionable section of the city and then, to the west, began the streets where the poor lived.

"It was in this room it happened."

What dreams, hopes, ambitions. Sometimes it had seemed to me, when as a young man I sat at the window of that room, that each person who passed along the street below, under the light, shouted his secret up to me.

I was myself and still I fled out of myself. It seemed to me that I went into the others.

What dreams! What egoism! I had thought then, on such evenings, that I could tell all of the stories of all the people of America. I would get them all, understand them, get their stories told.

And then came the night when it happened.

But what happened? It is the thing so hard to explain. It is however, the thing every young man and woman in the world will understand.

I had been working so long, so long. Oh how many thousand, hundreds of thousands of words put down.

Trying for something.

To escape out of old minds, old thoughts, put into my head by others, into my own thoughts, my own feelings.

Out of the others, the many, many others, who had worked in words, to have got so much I wanted but to be freed from them.

To at last go out of myself, truly into those others, the others I met constantly in the streets of the city, in the office where I then worked; the others, remembered out of my childhood in an American small town.

To be myself and yet, at the same time, the others.

And then, on a day, late in the afternoon of a day, I had come home to that room. I sat at a desk in a corner of the room. I wrote.

There was a story of another human, quite outside myself, truly told.

The story was one called "Hands." It was about a poor little man, beaten, pounded, frightened by the world in which he lived into something oddly beautiful.

The story was written that night in one sitting. No word of it ever changed. I wrote the story and got up. I walked up and down in that little narrow room. Tears flowed from my eyes.

"It is solid," I said to myself. "It is like a rock. It is there. It is put down."

There was, I'm sure, an upsurge of pride.

"See, at last I have done it. It is true. There it is."

In those words, scrawled on the sheets of paper, it is accomplished.

I am quite sure that on that night, when it happened in that room, when for the first time I dared whisper to myself, perhaps sobbing, that I had found it, my vocation, I knelt in the darkness and muttered words of gratitude to God.

That I had been on the right track, that I dared hope.

Pride, exaltation, all mixed with a new and great humbleness.

"It happened in that room.

"There I found my vocation.

"It is what we all want.

"All of this frantic search for wealth, for fame, position in life. It is all nothing.

"What we want, everyone of us, is our own vocation.

"It is the world hunger."

The above words going through my mind as I stood at the door of a shabby room in a shabby rooming house years later with my wife.

Remembering all my failures since that night when I alone there in that room found, for the first time, my own vocation.

Getting for the first time belief in self.

I must have muttered words to the landlady, taken my wife's arm, hurried out of that house, feeling deeply the shame of my many failures since that, the greatest moment of my life.

When I found . . . what every man and woman in the world wants . . . a vocation.

Winesburg, Ohio
After Twenty Years

by

Waldo Frank

S HERWOOD ANDERSON wrote his most famous book about
a generation ago; and it reveals a Mid-American world that
already then was a generation dead. A full half century
therefore divides the mind that reads the book today from
the life it portrays. Since, from this adequate perspective,
the work stands firm in its form, true in its livingness, strong
in its light upon our present, it is clear that "Winesburg,
Ohio" is a classic.

I had not re-read the book since it was published. Many of
its chapters were mailed to me in his own writing by Anderson himself, who then lived in Chicago and worked for an
advertising house near Jackson Boulevard. I still see the long
sprawling potent hand on the cheap paper, feel the luminous
life what swelled miraculously from it. I recall sending him
back one story which I wished to publish in *The Seven Arts,*
because it was written down totally without commas; a few
days later, it came back to me with commas sedulously
spaced after each fourth or fifth word, irrespective of meaning. I had no doubt of the significance of this prose; otherwise, in 1916 I should not with such assurance have entitled
my first essay on Anderson "Emerging Greatness"; but I
know now that accidentals like the handwriting and the
punctuation somewhat obscured for me, as the man's home-

spun did for many, the actual lineaments of this clear art. It is a dangerous hazard to re-read, after twenty-five years, a book involved in the dreams and fervors of one's youth; it is a blessing when that book stands forth from the test a rediscovery . . . indeed a prophecy and an illumination.

The first impressive realization that came to me with my re-reading was that "Winesburg" has form. The book as a whole has form; and most of the stories have form: the work is an integral creation. The form is lyrical. It is not related, even remotely, to the aesthetic of Chekhov; nor to that of Balzac, Flaubert, Maupassant, Tolstoy, Melville. These masters of the short story used the narrative or dramatic art: a linear progression rising to a peak or an immediate complex of character-forces impinging upon each other in a certain action that fulfilled them and rounded the story. For an analogy to the aestheic of the Winesburg tales, one must go to music, perhaps to the songs that Schubert featly wove from old refrains; or to the lyric art of the Old Testament psalmists and prophets in whom the literary medium was so allied to music that their texts have always been sung in the synagogues. The "Winesburg" design is quite uniform: a theme-statement of a character with his mood, followed by a recounting of actions that are merely variations on the theme. These variations make incarnate what has already been revealed to the reader; they weave the theme into life by the always subordinate confrontation of other characters (usually one) and by an evocation of landscape and village. In some of the tales, there is a secondary theme-statement followed by other variations. In a few, straight narrative is attempted; and these are the least successful.

This lyric, musical form has significance, and the tales' contents make it clear. But it is important, first, to note that the cant judgment of Sherwood Anderson as a naive, almost illiterate storyteller (a judgment which he himself encouraged with a good deal of nonsense about his literary innocence) is false. The substance of "Winesburg" is impressive, is alive, because it has been superbly *formed*. There are occasional superficial carelessnesses of language; on the whole, the prose is perfect in its selective economy and in its melodious flow; the choice of details is stript, strong, sure; the movement is an unswerving musical fulfillment of the already stated theme. Like Schubert, and like the Old Testament storytellers, the author of "Winesburg" comes at the end of a psychological process; is a man with an inherited culture and a deeply assimilated skill. He is a type of the achieved artist.

The theme of the tales taken as a whole follows the same pattern as the individual "chapters"—although less precisely. "Hands," the first chapter, tells of Adolph Myers, alias Wing Biddlebaum, the unfortunate schoolteacher with sensitive, wandering, caressing hands, who gets into trouble because his loving touch upon his pupils is misinterpreted by a half-wit boy and the crude obscene men of the town. Because the tale is concretely, poetically realized, its symbolism is true; and because this symbolism is not intellectualized, not schematized, it would be false to tear it from its flesh and blood texture. Suffice it to say that the story suggests the tragic ambivalence of hands, which is the fate of all the characters of Winesburg. Hands, at the turn of the century, were making machines, making all sorts of things ("the thing is in the saddle";), making the world that was unmaking the tender, sensitive, intimate lives of the folk in their villages and farms. Hands are made for loving; but hands making mechanical things grow callous, preoccupied . . . fail at love. The second story is a straight variant of the theme: here, it is not the hand, the maker, that goes wrong; it is *thought,* which Doctor Reefy turns into written words—ineffectual scraps of wisdom jotted down, that become paper pills cluttering his pocket. The third chapter, "Mother," completes the theme-statement. Woman, the creator, the lover: the principle incarnate in Wing Biddlebaum's hands and in Doctor Reefy's thoughts, states the theme centrally. The form of the mother, frustrate, lonely, as last desperate, pervades the variations that make the rest of the book: a continuity of variation swelling, swirling into the corners and crannies of the village life; and at length closing in the mother's death, in the loss forever of the $800

which Elizabeth Willard had kept for twenty years to give
her son his start away from Winesburg, and in the son's
wistful departure. "He thought of little things—"as the train
pulled out; they have become motes and beams carrying a
distant sun to the reader.

I have spoken of suggested symbols. Suggestion, if you
will *indirection*, is the quality of this lyric form; and no
more *direct* expression could have been devised for a book
which so precisely portrays a world avid for the expression
of eternal truths and forced, by the decay of its old cultural
foundation, to seek truth anarchically, hopelessly, indirectly.

It has become a critical commonplace that Winesburg
faithfully portrays the midwest village of two thousand souls
during the post-civil war pre-motor age. Let us look. . . . No
even bearably married couple is to be found in Winesburg;
there are few marriages in the book, and these without
exception are described as the harnessing together of strangers by the bondage of sex or a morality hostile to the spirit.
There is no communion with children. There is no fulfilled
sex life, sex being an obsession, a frustration and a trap.
There is no normal sociability between men and women:
souls lonely as carnivorae for once in their lives burst into
melodic plaint to one another, and lapse into solipsistic
silence. There is indeed more muttering than talk. There is
no congregated worship, and no strength to organized religion except in the sense of a strong barrier; as in the piteous
tales of the Reverend Hartman who sins by knocking a
piece from his stained-glass church window (part of the
figure of Christ) in order to gaze at the body of Belle Robinson in bed. There is almost no joy, beyond the momentary
joy of contemplating nature. And the most mature of the
characters, Doctor Reefy, Seth Richmond, Elizabeth Willard, the Rev. Hartman, et al., do not evolve beyond a sharp
negation of the things that *are*, in favor of a nebulous dream
of "life."

Now, these omissions are purposive; and as aesthetically
true as they are factually false. The author's art, perhaps
unconsciously to himself, traces the frontier of emotional

and spiritual action which, in that deliquescence of an agrarian culture which was rotten long ere it was ripe, was a line of *decay,* a domain of deprivation. In those very institutions and traditions which had been the base of the world's health, Winesburg was found wanting.

The positive substance of the book is the solitariness and struggle of the soul which has lost its ancestral props: the energy of the book is the release from these old forms into a subliminal search for new ones. The farms of Robert Frost's "North of Boston" are also peopled by broken, lonely lives; but their despair is hard, heroic. The folk of Winesburg are soft in a tenderness, in a nebulous searchfulness, that have gone farther in decay than the still standing families and churches of Frost's New England. In all the book, only irony—the author's irony—is hard.

This trait of Sherwood Anderson has been too little recognized. Consider the acrid irony in "Nobody Knows," where sex fulfillment ends in the boy's cowardly sigh of relief that "she hasn't got anything on me. Nobody knows"; in "The Awakening," that turns a moment of mystical insight into a brutal, humiliating sexual frustration; in "The Untold Lie" (one of the great stories of the world); in the chapters of Jesse Bentley, "the man of God" who is transformed by the sling of his grandchild, David, into a clumsy, puny, ineffectual Goliath. This hardness of irony in the author points to his spiritual transcendence over his subjects. Anderson has inherited intact a strength long since vaporized in Winesburg—and yet the heritage of Winesburg. His sureness of vision and of grasp enable him to incarnate in a form very precise the inchoate emotions of his people. To portray the deliquescence of America's agrarian culture beneath the impact of the untamed machine age required a man spiritually advanced beyond that culture's death. This is a law of art (and of ethic) ignored by the hardboiled Hemingway school, who depict their gangsters *on the level of the gangsters.*

Sherwood Anderson liked to think of himself as a primitive or neo-primitive artist; as a naive unlettered storyteller. The truth is, that he belonged at the end of a cultural process, and shares the technical perfection which, within the limits of the culture's forms, only the terminal man achieves. One book was the pabulum of these people: the Bible. And a Testamental accent and vision modulate every page of Sherwood Anderson's great story. Moreover, the nebulosity of these poor souls' search is an end, a chaos *after* a world. That world was already drooping when it crossed the ocean; it had been, in England, a world of revealed religion and sacramental marriage, of the May dance and the sense of each man's life as mystery and mission. It lives in the past of Winesburg; it has become a beat and a refrain in the blood. In the actual experience of these men and women, it is a recidivism, a lapse away into organic echoes. Thus, of revealed religion and sacramental marriage, of the structures of social and personal responsibilities, nothing remains on the record but the memory and the dynamic yearning. Life has become a Prompter with the text of the dialogue and even the stage missing.

In sum, Sherwood Anderson is a mature voice singing a culture at its close; singing it with the technical skill of, literally, the *past master*. What in Winesburg, Ohio, of the year 1900 was authentic? The old strong concept of marriage? No: only the inherited knowledge that the embrace of man and woman must create a sacrament again. The old dogmas of the churches? No: only the inherited knowledge that there is God—even in sin, there is God; and that for want of a living Body formed of this new world, God is revealed in animistic gods of the corn, and even in the phallus. Thus the artist, distilling the eternal from the old doomed ways, becomes the prophet.

Sherwood Anderson's place at the end of a cultural cycle finds eloquent corroboration in the quality of his immediate imitators and disciples. Ernest Hemingway turned the nebulous seeking softness of the master's characters into a hardshell bravado. Winesburg's men and women are old souls, inheritors of a great Christian culture who have been abandoned and doomed to a progressive emptiness by the invasion of the unmastered Machine. (This is a process now at its nadir in the world.) In Anderson, however, these lives are transfigured by a mature and virile artist who is able to crystallize what is eternal in them as an aesthetic value. In Hemingway, an adolescent rationalizes the emptiness (which flatters his own) into a rhetorical terseness which flatters the emptiness of the reader; and the essential formlessness of the story is slicked up into plots borrowed from the thrillers. In Thomas Wolfe, the same formlessness becomes grandiose, the nebulosity becomes an elephantiasis, the yearning and lostness discreetly lyricized in Winesburg becomes a flatulent, auto-erotic *Ding an Sich*. What is vital since Anderson in American letters (a great deal, varying from such men as Faulkner and Caldwell through Hart Crane to such young poets as Kenneth Patchen and Muriel Rukeyser) is independent of the Winesburg tradition. But that is another story. . . .

The perfect readability of this book within our agonizing world proves the potential that lived—needing only to be transfigured—within a world already gone when Winesburg was written. Here are intrinsically great stories: as great as any in our language. The author, intellectually bound to the decadance of the agrarian age that he revealed, proves in himself a vital spirit, a creative promise that are ours. The village of these queer men beating the innocent bystander to prove they are not queer, of these sex-starved women running naked through the summer rain, was after all pregnant of the Great Tradition. The tender and humbly precise artist who painted these portraits bespoke the Tradition's still unimagined future.

May 1941.

Anderson in Chicago

by

Harry Hansen

Sherwood Anderson came to Chicago when the very air was electric; rarely has a locality provided so well the setting for the ferment of ideas and the development of personality. That was the period when Theodore Dreiser was still sold under-the-counter; when Harriet Monroe was scraping together a modest endowment in order to print Lindsay, Frost, Robinson and H. D.; when Edgar Lee Masters wrote verse under two names for *Reedy's Mirror* and practiced law with Clarence Darrow; when Harriet Moody opened her house and her purse to poets from Ireland and Hoboken; when Maurice Browne began producing Greek plays; when Floyd Dell had inherited the *Post* from Francis Hackett, and Carl Sandburg was seen wearing his flowing black tie. It was small-town, Midwest, but the talk was not provincial. Nordau, Stirner, Schnitzler, Freud, Anatole France, Shaw, the post-impressionists, Strindberg, the whole Huneker table of contents, and, after Ben Hecht arrived with "The Idiot" under his arm, Dostoevski—these and many others were the topics of debate.

It goes without saying that if Sherwood Anderson's individuality had not been well established at this time he might have been swayed by the prevailing winds and aped styles,

but the evidence is that his mind was formed and he knew
what he wanted to write. His Ohio roots went deep, and
although it is quite likely that "Winesburg, Ohio" had
scenes and characters that he saw from his windows in Cass
Street, its beginnings lie in the small-town earth. He already
had his way of brooding over people; he had that wish for
getting past the surface attitudes of human beings; he enjoyed talking to the plain fellows, streetcar motormen, store-
keepers; and he had that intuitive feeling for words and
rhythms that was to make his prose a thing apart. His happy
discovery of "The Bible in Spain" at the hands of a schoolteacher had occurred in Ohio, and that elation was typical of
his attitude toward "the tools of the craft" all his life.

Of course the Chicago group was useful to him as stimula-
tion and audience. Friends did try to make him shape up his
early novels, which were neither good writing nor good
merchandise, but their failure proved that Anderson couldn't
compromise with accepted patterns and had not yet found
his natural vehicle. I never saw Sherwood in action in what
had been Thornstein Veblen's old store near Jackson Park—
being in Europe most of the time—but the tale is that Sherwood would sit silently, listening with glowing eyes, until he
got a chance to talk. Then he would pull out a manuscript
and read and read, or stalk up and down the room and talk
himself out. The achievements of that Chicago circle belie
the tradition that writers who talk a lot don't write.

Then, as later, he talked about tools, craftsmanship, the
need of a man using his hands and producing something
complete, as men did once in the harness shop and at the
cabinetmaker's. But what was still possible for a writer was
impossible for the harness maker—the competitive market
had ruined him. Anderson's argument signified his disgust
with standardization and his love of original work. The
whole Chicago circle supported this movement toward free
expression. Dreiser's influence was powerful among them;
Margaret Anderson, a good evangelist, talked Stein and
Joyce incessantly; the free verse poets, now becoming prolific,
were in full revolt against conventional poetry. The "crudity"

that Anderson defended was not a bar to appreciation.

Dreiser, who was in and out of Chicago, made the greatest impression on Anderson, who approved his rejection of the conventional plot. He spoke of Dreiser as "an honest workman, always impersonal, never a trickster," and praised his short stories because they were bits of life, not plotted situations. Anderson recognized the authentic, midwestern character of Dreiser's writing and valued it as free from the European influences visible in classic Americans—later called colonial. The situation in which Dreiser found himself also appealed to Anderson. Dreiser went to New York to edit *Delineator* and to buy stories with which he was out of sympathy. Anderson wrote advertising copy and sold campaigns for Critchfield, while inwardly contemptuous of the whole go-getter attitude. Neither author remained long at the treadmill, but both were competent in their jobs.

Anderson, like Carl Sandburg, could be a most stimulating companion alone and get completely lost in a crowd. I cherish memories of quiet talks with him in basement restaurants, sought out for the food or the red wine; more often because Anderson had found the human side interesting. He would have talked with the owner, or his wife, about their homely cares, their inner hopes. He knew people either desired something very much and couldn't get it, or that desire was dead; and he was most sensitive to the promptings of appetite, hunger and "the perpetual tragedy of unfulfillment." He was extremely aware of his hands as tools; in fact he was always conscious of his body as an instrument of expression. His sensuousness was not mere appetite, but a sort of basic means of communication and understanding with all human beings. He let people talk without interruption, not so much to hear the words they used as to speculate what lay behind them, for he felt that many of the words are not innately our own but inexact devices for our thoughts. When he wrote he did not try to reproduce the vernacular but used simple words that sounded well and seemed accurate to him. Thus he did not fall into the habit of reporting that gives monotony to so much of our naturalistic fiction.

Anderson often talked technique, too, always with emphasis on the sense of life in fiction. He did not see why a story should be a full circle, meeting conventional expectations. In life, a man walked down the street, other men approached him along the route, talked with him and left again; he continued on, and when your interest in his particular situation ceased you let him go beyond your vision. You didn't see him married, dead and buried—interrupted in his natural progress. Today this is not news, but when Anderson talked it, it was worth a stiff debate. The Chicago group enjoyed controversy and every season brought a book or a poem that broke bonds anew. I suppose the decade of 1910-1920 was the most fertile and influential in American writing since the day of the stalwarts in the middle 19th century. After 1920 individuals began to move to Paris and New York. By that time Sherwood Anderson had found himself, and although his writing remained "opaque" to some to the end of his days, he had helped win a victory for honest expression that will last our time.

Hello Towns

The world weeps itself in the chain of the mist;
it lowers a curtain, a faltering fountain.
As a man is a town and the town is a map,
the horizon's a secret in the midst of the rain.

Saying — "Hello!" this wall is the world;
older than commerce which fashioned us here.
Smoking from chimneys; smoking from pipes,
men from old countries completed these towns.

This is the village, the place we all know;
boasting a library, a socialist, a red.
But to whom will it matter if we can discuss it
if something is missing in the mind and the heart.

Saying — "Hello!" But there's no one to greet you;
the suburbs are factories frozen with filth.
But they nod as you pass, for you never have left it;
you never have left it and you never returned.

—HARRY ROSKOLENKO

The Philosophy of
Sherwood Anderson

by

Julius W. Friend

T HE APPROACH of Sherwood Anderson to ultimate questions, to what metaphysicians call the problems of being, of
knowledge, of ethics etc., was not that of the abstract rea-
soner. Anderson did arrive at conclusions, but his ideas
were drawn directly from his feeling for the world of his
experience. Hart Crane reports a conversation in which
Anderson said, "I am mighty little interested in discussions
of what a man's place in the scheme of things may be. After
all, there is the fact of life. Its story wants telling and singing." This story and its song are embodied in a sizeable
number of novels, stories, plays, poems and articles. Taken
together they represent a surprisingly unified view. From this
material it is possible to extract in cold and formal words
the intent of a philosophy. The objection that in the case of
Anderson such a philosophy is a matter of intuitive feeling
rather than deliberate thought is irrelevant. We are here
concerned with the results, no matter how they may have
been arrived at.

The best general characterization of Anderson's philosophy is to call it mystical. His mysticism, however, is not
the Christian or Buddhist variety which denies the world
and the senses in favor of an ineffable vision of God. It might

better be called an earth mysticism, which accepts life, the
life of the teeming earth, the life of the senses, as well as the
life of the spirit, with something approaching the same kind
of ecstasy as that of the Christian mystics. Such an acceptance is not a rational conviction, but a whole-souled reach-
ing out and yearning. The vision must wait upon inspiration,
and when inspiration fails, the vision fails miserably. But
when it succeeds its effect is overwhelming and the report
of it is "dramatic, poignant, sometimes even a little hys-
terical." We are constantly being told by Anderson that
"Nothing natural is unbeautiful," "Nothing natural is
repulsive." "Flesh is sweet and unashamed," "Life may be a
lovely thing, only if lives dare surrender to it simply, freely."

Conversely, evil is to be understood as that which thwarts
or baffles life. It is always the denial of vitality. In the story
"Unused," May Edgely "was afraid of everything human."
In "I'm a Fool," the boy finds beauty but is barred from it by
his own lies. Time and again the theme recurs in the novels
of the deadening discipline imposed by the machine. Failures
for Anderson, are likely to be conventionally successful men
and women who are precluded from growing by a too easy
fruition, who in climbing to success have to shut their hearts
to deeper and wider understanding. I doubt whether Sherwood Anderson recognized any other kind of failure than the
failure to open one's eyes and heart to the ecstatic current
of life.

Since it was Mother Earth rather than God the Father to
whom Anderson tendered his worship, it is not extraordinary
that he should have employed sex symbolism to the extent
that he did. Sex in Anderson's writings includes what the
physiologists recognize as sex, but this aspect of sex is by
itself of little interest. Sex is the symbol of whatever lives,
grows or creates; it is the very spirit of affirmation which
bursts the bonds of the fixed and static. With such beliefs it
was to have been expected that Anderson would be called a
Freudian, and no doubt Anderson toyed with this notion
himself. But between him and Freud there is a vast difference. Freud derived all human values from sexual desire at

the level of physiology. Anderson regarded physiological sex only as a familiar symbol of creativity. With Freud the higher depends upon the lower. For Anderson the *eros* is diffused over the universe. Its acute centering, as in the case of animal desire, is but one of its many and various phenomena.

In the story "Hands" he presents a picture of the school-teacher, a man in whom the love impulse was not centered, as it is with most persons; who wished to express himself, to communicate himself to the boys whom he taught. He is depicted as a rare and noble soul, tragically misunderstood by the villagers as a pervert and hounded out of town. Compare this portrait with that of Leonardo da Vinci as drawn by Freud. In that book, with the help of *ad hoc* theories and far-fetched evidence, Freud proves to his own satisfaction that Leonardo's genius depended upon sex perversion. Between the ideas of Freud and Anderson there is superficial similarity and a depth of difference. Anderson recognized no dualism of the sensual and the spiritual. He would not have admitted that a worship of Mother Earth precludes God the Father. Indeed, he once remarked to me during a discussion of religion, "You will have to say that I have never let God down."

It is plain that such a monistic philosophy could not end in a trivial hedonism, no matter how much it might endorse the sensual. Anderson proclaimed and approved the counsel to "eat, drink and be merry," but certainly not because "tomorrow we may die." The pleasures of the senses were never very absorbing to him, and he was as much convinced of the realities beyond them as any Platonic philosopher. Indeed all his successful tales are concerned with those rare flashes of value which occasionally light up humdrum existence, and which alone make us believe that life is aimed at something important. Intoxication with the wine of creativity and not the leisurely tasting of its less heady moments was his obsession. It is curious therefore that he should ever have been confused with the school of naturalism, (or as it is miscalled, realism). Anderson never troubled to observe and note down details which had no relevance for his vision. Experience

yielded important insights, the details required might be
selected or invented. If one must label this kind of writing,
it is symbolism rather than naturalism. Similarly t is a ludi-
crous, critical error to put him alongside writers such as
Sinclair Lewis whose books about the American small town
are a protest against intellectual narrowness. Sherwood
Anderson is never a debunker. The small town compares
favorably with the big city for almost the same reason that
the debunkers employ to belittle it: in the big city, life
becomes rootless and abstract.

It was not that Sherwood Anderson was scornful of ideas.
Many of the men with whom he formed close associations
were of the intellectual type. It was rather that he was
instinctively suspicious of the rationalistic approach not only
because it ends so often in conclusions which are palpably
absurd, but also because the direction of abstract thought
leads away from contact with vivid earth. He believed that
the rich welling substance of life is to be found only in the
abundance of the actual world as it shows itself to immediate
feeling, and that it is lost when rational processes work over
memories. So the realm of values seemed to him to be an
everlasting Now which human perception, caught as it is in
the flux of time, fumbles for and usually misses.

"You must understand that it is my desire to communicate to you something of the Now, the present."
And,
"I have a passionate hunger to take a bite out of the
Now. The Now is a country to discover which, to be the
pioneer in which I would give all thought, all memories,
all hope. My ship has but skirted the shores of that
country."
These gleams of value which constitute the significant
element because they proceed from life itself are occult to the
rationalist, to him who has closed his life by success, and,
indeed, they are with difficulty and seldom presented even to
the devotee. Anderson claimed to be only a very modest
explorer, feeling "with nervous and uncertain hands for the
form of things concealed in the darkness." He tells us,

"We have not approached the time when we may speak to each other, but in the mornings sometimes I have heard, echoing far off, the sound of a trumpet."

Anderson's mysticism, however, did not usually carry him into such eery metaphysical matters. But it suffers no diminution when it is focused upon human relationships. He believed that in every contact between two personalities a third thing emerges which is not the property of either person, but the property of that relationship. Thus every person who encounters another, creates a value different from that which he might establish with still another person. The world of human relationships becomes one of infinite richness for those who have the eyes to see it. Such values are not to be classified by ordinary generic terms; they are not logical relations such as father-son, lover-mistress, brother-sister; each is unique, the unique resultant of two personalities each itself unique. The flavor of what in denotative language one calls 'personal relationship' is hardly to be described but must be felt. No wonder, Anderson, cognizant of this embarrassment of riches, found his task of communication so difficult and hesitating. Moreover, such creation as emerges from the contact of two personalities, he believed to emerge also from the contact of a human being with things that he loves—and perhaps between animals and the growing things of the earth. Even dumb materiality reaches out to form a pattern of value with other things and creatures. He was especially intrigued by the man who has "a feeling" for his material—the inventor of machines whom he declared not to be really interested in making something useful which would work to make more useful goods. Thus he saw the inventor as a tragic figure since his labors of love eventuated in crushing out love by making life mechanical and dead.

In this world of indefinitely rich potential contact, Anderson recognized that some things and some persons are good for each other, and some bad. Again, good and bad are interpreted as meaning life enhancing and life denying. Perhaps it would be better to say that certain contacts are demanded

for a human being if he or she is to live and grow. Love
between men and women is the most obvious of these needs,
though it stood in Anderson's mind as a symbol of all needs,
and especially for those less well understood communions of
the spirit which are so hard to describe.

Nor was Anderson insensible to the value of communion
which emerges when a group of persons unite for a purpose
in which they fiercely believe. I think it was for this reason
alone that he ever became interested in the labor movement.
He once told me that there was something "marvelous" about
a strike. But the marvel to him consisted wholly in the concrete actions and attitudes of sacrifice and cooperation which
the strikers show under stress. He was not interested, save
casually, in the outcome—still less in the economic problem
involved. Neither did he indulge in the current sentimental-
ity which identifies virtue with the workers and vice with the
managers. Anderson never classified human beings according to economic strata. He was too shrewd to be taken in by
rationalistic dogma. If he chose to write principally about
unsuccessful and even socially degraded people it was only
because he wished to emphasize that what makes life significant has little or nothing to do with conventional judgments. He declared that "only the few know the sweetness
of the twisted apples."

Nevertheless, Anderson's literary bias in favor of the
lowly and the 'under privileged' was interpreted according to
the fashion of the moment as linking him with the so-called
proletarian school, and because of his prestige he was fastened
upon by various leftist political groups. But I believe it is safe
to say that he never went further in this sort of activity than
to allow his name to be printed on committee letterheads.
With all his faith in the value of human communion he seldom confused it with any doctrinaire scheme of organization.
His sureness of intuition extricated him from every "ism."
Political people, he believed, whether they admit it to themselves or not, really want to push somebody else around, to
inflict their ideas on others. Whereas, it is a major premise of
Anderson's philosophy that human personality is sacred and

should be inviolate. I think this to have been at the bottom of his dislike of political activities and his frequent disclaimer of interest in politics.

Yet Sherwood Anderson had faith in American democracy! His faith was not literal but essential; it had nothing to do with the rhetoric of candidates running for office. Rather like Walt Whitman, he went to the heart of the matter, to the values on which democracy is built and which alone make it worth preserving. Anderson firmly held his belief in the sanctity of human personality, without which the machinery of democratic government is a ridiculous merry-go-round. At the same time his belief in the value of the person could not lead to a rampant individualism. His belief results in the community of persons, which is strong because it is bound together by bonds of concrete and multiform feelings.

In so far as it can be abstracted from his writings and conversation, one can sum up his philosophy as a mystical acceptance of all that is affirmative, and as a faith that there is overwhelming significance in mortal experience proceeding from infinite potential communions—from "many marriages." He himself would have been the last to claim that his vision was complete and well-rounded. On the contrary, he tells us on innumerable occasions that his vision is hesitant and his grasp of it fumbling and uncertain. So it would hardly be fair to abstract a philosophical position, as I have attempted, and then criticize it as a complete philosophy. I know that in the hands of another who did not have Sherwood Anderson's intuitive grasp it might appear that the monism of content and form is too easily effected; that it is not clear how so much worship of the Earth does not "let God down." It might be charged that it is romantic and sentimental to place no limits on any affirmation, that it is over-optimistic to hold that every positive act is right. It could be said that the evil which results from actions motivated by good is a moral complexity which Anderson seldom took into account. Thus when John Webster walks out on his family to go away with Natalie his action is not presented as immoral, yet it is hard for the reader to see it otherwise. But

Sherwood Anderson was not writing a tract in "Many Marriages." He can hardly be blamed for concentrating on one facet of existence. He was obsessed with the glory of life and equipped with the ability to find it in places where we would never look. It was neither his business nor his interest to think in terms of inner checks. He knew as we all do that outer checks, no matter how necessary, are bad. He was a yea-sayer who looked into mystery of experience perhaps as deeply as anyone who has ever written.

By the same token he has more to teach philosophers than they have to teach him. His conviction that rational categories drawn from memory of experience end by simplifying and caricaturing the source, from which they are drawn, remains a salutary lesson. Necessary as such generalizations may be—and they were necessary to Anderson himself—they need to be continually reformulated in the light of immediate feeling. He himself used continually to discard one formulation and go back to form another. It was for the reason that he knew, just as his Dr. Reefy in Winesburg knew, that conclusions, once arrived at and kept, form themselves into hard paper pills filling up the pockets of the mind, and after they have accumulated for a while, must be thrown away.

Letters to Van Wyck Brooks

I FIRST met Sherwood Anderson in the late winter of 1917 at the office of *The Seven Arts* in New York. I think it was Waldo Frank who brought him into the magazine, of which Frank and I and James Oppenheim were editors. Paul Rosenfeld and Randolph Bourne were also of the circle, and we all became good friends; and I believe that *The Seven Arts* published the first of the Winesburg stories. Sherwood was still at that time in business, but he had written several novels, along with a great number of short stories; and he was eager to break his connection with business and establish himself as a writer. As he said in one of his letters, "I want to quit working for a living and go wander for five years in our towns." I can remember how struck I was by his fresh healthy mind and his true Whitmanian feeling for comradeship, his beautiful humility, his lovely generosity and the "proud conscious innocence" of his nature. This was his own phrase for Mark Twain's mind at the time when he was writing "Huckleberry Finn," and it goes for Sherwood also. He was the most natural of men, as innocent as any animal or flowering tree.

For six or seven years we saw much of each other, and these letters are the record of our friendship. They are especially interesting because these were the years during which he was discovering himself and his world. He was, as

he says, "setting out on new roads," tasting the "Mid-
America" that was his land, "the place between mountain
and mountain"—touching it, catching its scent, listening,
seeing; and his letters bring back the feeling of that time,
when we were all of us groping and lonely. We were all
trying to understand the nature of America, turning away
from "European culture," and we all felt, as Sherwood says,
that we were "struggling in a vacuum"—we had that "queer
sense of carving a stone" that would be "cast into a stagnant
sea." Well I remember these feelings, which Sherwood
expresses; and I remember too what a boon it was to have
a meeting-place at *The Seven Arts*. While most of us were
Easterners, we felt that the heart of America lay in the
West; and Sherwood was the essence of his West. He was
full of Lincoln and especially of Mark Twain, and he wanted
to sell me Twain, as he said in a letter. I was writing "The
Ordeal of Mark Twain," and he was anxious for me to understand him; and after I published the book he showed me
clearly where my study had fallen short. I had failed to
write the most important chapter, in which I should have
praised "Huckleberry Finn." I was too much concerned with
the psychological problem, and the psychologist inhibited the
poet in me. I regretted this as much as Sherwood, who loved
Mark Twain above all writers. The last time I saw Sherwood,
about 1939, we were dining in New York in a semipublic
room. On the wall hung a life-sized photograph of Mark
Twain, sitting in his rocking chair on the piazza at Redding.
Sherwood looked up at it and smiled as he said, "There was
a lovely man."

Sherwood bewailed Mark Twain's going East, among men
from "barren hills and barren towns"; and he wrote to me,
"A man cannot be a pessimist who lives near a brook or a
cornfield." He never lost his happiness or his faith, for he
knew where he belonged and he loved it. He brooded over
his own country and sang it. He sang it least well perhaps
in the "Mid-American Chants," which was rather a matrix of
poetry than poetry proper. But his short stories were poems.
They were certainly acrid at moments, but there he was

always the poet. He suggests in these letters that I questioned his quality now and then, though he said that I was entitled to my personal taste. Well, the only question I felt regarded his novels, and I may have been quite mistaken. I only regretted that he wrote novels when he had a gift for story-telling that was, in its different way, like Chekhov's; for I never could feel that his novels were as good as his stories, and he was the most enthralling teller of tales. Never can I forget an evening, in 1937, which he spent at my house in Westport. For two hours he told stories about the folks at Marion, while we all listened like a three years' child.

VAN WYCK BROOKS.

Chicago—1918?

Brooks:

I cannot resist the temptation to write you a letter induced by a talk Waldo Frank and I had last evening. The talk drifted to Mark Twain and your attitude toward him. Something Waldo said gave me the notion that your digging into his work had made you a little ill—that you had seen, perhaps too clearly, his dreadful vulgarity and cheapness.

Of course your book cannot be written in a cheerful spirit. In facing Twain's life you face a tragedy. How could the man mean what he does to us if it were not a tragedy. Had the man succeeded in breaking through he would not have been a part of us. Can't you take it that way?

America a land of children—broken off from the culture of the world. Twain there—a part of that. Then the coming of industrialism. The putting of the child into the factory.

Mark Twain was a factory child. I am that. I can however stand off and look at him. When it would be second rate and unmanly to weep concerning myself I can think of him. For his very failure I love him. He was maimed, hurt, broken. In some way he got caught up by the dreadful cheap smartness, the shrillness that was a part of the life of the country, that is still its dominant note.

I don't want you to get off Twain. I want your mind on it. Please do not lose courage, do not be frightened away by the muck and ugliness of it.

For the Americans of the future there can be no escape. They have got to, in some way, face themselves. Your book, about the man they love and in a dumb way understand, will help mightily. I do want you to write that book.

Sherwood Anderson

Van Wyck Brooks
Dear Brooks:

I am glad you are going to get at Twain. It is absurd that he should have been translated as an artist by a man like Howells or that fellow Paine. There is something about him no one has got hold of. He belonged out here in the Middle West and was only incidentally a writer.

I've a notion that after Twain passed under the influence of Howells and others of the east he began to think of himself as a writer and lost something of his innocence. Should not one go to Huck Finn for the real man, working out of a real people?

Several years ago I tried to write a story concerning Twain. It never got to anything but I have a copy of the attempt in my desk. There is a character in the story—the old cheese maker from Indiana that I will sometime make the central figure in a real story. He is Twain's type of man.

It is odd what literary connections one makes. In my own mind I have always coupled Mark Twain with George Borrow. I get the same quality of honesty in them, the same wholesome disregard of literary precedent.

Lanes* have decided to go ahead with my cornfield songs. I call them Mid-American chants. Then I am going to publish the Winesburg tales—some two dozen of them in a book under the title Winesburg. When I came to look at my novel Mary Cochran—written several years ago—it didn't suit me. I shall hold it back for more work.

* John Lane published several of Anderson's Books.

One has to realize that although there is truth in the Winesburg things there is another big story to be done. We are no longer the old America. Those are tales of farming people. We've got a new people now. We are a growing, shifting, changing thing. Our life in our factory towns intensifies. It becomes at the same time more ugly and more intense.

God damn it Brooks I wish my books would sell for one reason. I want to quit working for a living and go wander for five years in our towns. I want to be a factory hand again and wander from place to place. I want my frame to unbend from the desk and to go look and listen to this new thing.

My songs are going to be widely abused and perhaps rightly. I'm a poor enough singer. But there is a song here and it has been muffed. Masters might get it but he has too keen a quality of hate.

It makes me ill when I think how little I get done and the years hurrying along but I suppose we all know that sickness. I would like you to know I appreciate your interest in my efforts. The fact that you are interested is one of the bright spots. The quality of your mind I have always thought one of the really bully things of my generation.

I'll get to New York again some time. When I do I hope to see and talk with you.

Sherwood Anderson

59 W. Schiller St.

I'll send you the Twain thing to read if I can find it for the sake of the cheese maker.

1918

Dear Brooks:

Waldo Frank gave me Charnwood's Lincoln when he was out here. Today there came from my bookseller your America's Coming of Age—I had not read it.

You and Charnwood are so oddly in the same spirit that I have been thinking of you. At lunch I read your essay on Highbrows and Lowbrows.

The conviction grows in me that you are seeing and thinking with extraordinary clearness but I am constantly puzzled by something.

I get in some odd way a sense of the fact that you want constantly to write of men like Twain and Whitman but draw back from their inperfections, their looseness of thought, their vulgarities.

The thought that was in my mind at lunch and that I want to put over to you may have no essential value as it may be an old thought to you.

Is not the tendency to dislike these men's imperfections— if you have it—an inclination in you to drift toward your own Highbrow classification?

I ask hesitatingly. I do not of course know.

I want you to write of Twain. I want to see that book come from you.

Surely the thing has to be undertaken as a labor of love and love should stomach imperfections.

I dare say that as you work you see little result from your work. You can't of course be popular. I believe however that you by some odd chance see the difficulties of the artistic tendency in the midst of American life more clearly than anyone else.

It is always and more than you realize worth while to men deeply involved and perhaps muddied by the looseness and vulgarity of life that you keep going ahead.

Your book is helpful to me as everything of yours I have ever seen is helpful.

S. Anderson

May 23rd, 1918

Dear Brooks:

I cannot resist an impulse I have to write to you again concerning your book—"America's Coming of Age." Are there any others of your books in which you also develop the theme you have here taken hold of so firmly?

The amazing thing to me about your mind Brooks is that you see so clearly what I did not suppose any man with a background such as I had thought of you as having could see.

I have myself understood that trenchant sadness of Lincoln, the rather childlike pessimism of Twain, the half sullen and dogmatic insistence on the part of Dreiser on the fight with Puritanism and Whitman's windy insistence on America. I thought I understood these things because I have lived in such a barren place, felt myself so futile, because I have really always felt a lack of strength to continue struggling in a vacuum and looked forward hopelessly to the time when some quirk of the mind would lead me to adopt finally some grotesque sectional attitude and spend myself uselessly on that.

When I talked to Waldo out here I felt in him a sense of background I have never had. I wondered if he knew the utter lack of background. It means so very much that you know and of course he must know also.

One works in an oddly futile way. This year, because I have been very tired after ten years of trying to stay among the men about me, to be part and parcel of them, and at the same time to build something a little permanent at odd moments.

One cannot surrender to the cheaper inclinations in writing, to miss perhaps the secondary approval of an ass like Mencken as his reward.

But then one gets this queer sense of carving a stone that will presently be cast into a stagnant sea, into the Sargasso Sea as you suggest.

I am very sure, after reading this book that you must be sad also, that you also must feel deeply the futility of things.

What I want to ask you is why you do not sympathize with me in such expressions as my essay An Apology for Crudity or my Chants? Where do I hit wrong?

In the chants I reached into my own personal muttering, half insane and disordered and tried to take out of them a little something ordered. You should see how I clutched at the ordered cornfield, insisted on them to myself, took them as about the only thing I could see.

I haven't the right to expect much from such mutterings but I have the right to expect that, having written this book I have just read, you would know what I was at.

Forgive me if I sink to the triviality of explanation. Your mind has won my honest respect. I do not so much seek your approval as I do your brotherhood.

May I say that for me yours is the first, the only note in American criticism that I have ever thought worth a damn. It is really and deeply understanding.

Sherwood Anderson

Do try to form the habit of writing me some of your thoughts occasionally. It is lonely out here.

My dear Brooks:

Your letter has stirred up a world of thought in me. It isn't Twain I'm thinking of but the profound truth of some of your own observations.

As far as Twain is concerned we have to remember the influences about him. Remember how he came into literature—the crude buffoon of the early days in the mining camps—the terrible cheap and second rate humor of much of Innocence Abroad. It seems to me that when he began he addressed an audience that gets a big laugh out of the braying of a jackass and without a doubt Mark often brayed at them. He knew that later. There was tenderness and subtility in Mark when he grew older.

You get the picture of him Brooks—the river man who could write going east and getting in with that New England crowd—the fellows from barren hills and barren towns. The best he got out of the bunch was Howells and Howells did Twain no good.

There's another point Brooks I can't help wishing Twain hadn't married such a good woman. There was such a universal inclination to tame the man—to save his soul as it were. Left alone I fancy Mark might have been willing to throw his soul overboard and then—ye gods what a fellow he might have been, what poetry might have come from him.

The big point is—it seems to me that this salvation of the soul business gets under everybody's skin. With artists it takes the form of being concerned with their occupation as writers. A struggle constantly goes on. Call the poet a poet and he is no longer the poet. You see what I mean.

There is a fellow like X. for example. He writes me long letters. His days are often made happy or miserable according to whether or not he is writing well.

Is it so important? What star dust we are. What does it matter?

The point is that I catch X. so often striving to say things in an unusual way. It makes me cringe. I want to beat him with my fists.

I pick on X. as an example because I love him and I know he feels deeply. He should write with a swing—weeping, praying and crying to the gods on paper instead of making sentences as he so often does.

Well now you see I'm coming around. The cultural fellows got hold of Mark. They couldn't hold him. He was too big and too strong. He brushed their hands aside.

But their words got into his mind. In the effort to get out beyond that he became a pessimist.

Now Brooks you know a man cannot be a pessimist who lives near a brook or a cornfield. When the brook chatters or at night when the moon comes up and the wind plays in the corn a man hears the whispering of the gods.

Mark got to that once—when he wrote Huck Finn. He forgot Howells and the good wife and everyone. Again he was the half savage, tender, god-worshiping, believing boy. He had proud conscious innocence.

I believe he wrote that book in a little hut on a hill on his farm. It poured out of him. I fancy that at night he came down from his hill stepping like a king—a splendid playboy, playing with rivers and men, ending on the Mississippi, on the broad river that is the great artery flowing out of the heart of the land.

Well Brooks I'm alone in a boat on that stream sometimes. The rhythm and swing of it is in some of my songs that are to be published next month. It sometimes gets into some of

the Winesburg things. I'll ride it some more perhaps. It
depends on whether or not I can avoid taking myself serious.
Whom the gods wish to destroy they first make dumb with
the notion of being a writer.

Waldo is coming out to spend a month with me.

Wish I could see you sometime this summer. I'll be in the
east for a month or more in June or July. Why couldn't you
come to the mountains and have a few days walk with me?

Sherwood Anderson

May 31, 1918

Dear Brooks:

I know of course what you mean and it is because you
have the clearsightedness to see that you are of such very
great value. American writers have a trick of doing something it is difficult at first to understand. They harden, ripen
out of time. Your notion of the stony field has signficance.
In such a field corn would come too soon to tassel. It would
turn yellow and produce no grain.

You can see for yourself how our critics produce that
peculiarly shallow effect. Dell goes that way, Mencken,
Hackett, and our newspaper men out here are peculiarly so.
Waldo can tell you of them.

It is probably true that the reason our men who are of
importance, Lincoln, Whitman, Twain, Dreiser etc., all
begin when they are almost old men is that they have to
spend so much of their lives putting down roots. The strength
goes into that. We have you see Lincoln producing a few
notable utterances, Whitman some clear stuff out of much
windiness; Twain, Huck Finn; Dreiser, Sister Carrie, etc.

Oddly enough you are the first man I have seen stoutly
at it trying to take the stones out of the field—to give the
roots a chance.

If you could get at Twain sympathetically and show how

and why he failed it would be lifting a great stone. He, now, you see, is just about to be accepted by the smart alecks as the great man. We shall be clubbed with his failures and the cheap things he did. His bad work will be glorified as it has been by Howells and others.

As for myself I think there is soil for the raising of a crop if the stones can be taken away. . . .

Your attitude toward my own efforts is generous and helpful. What I am trying to say to you in all this letter writing is aside from that but connected with it too.

Any work accomplished is a thing already half dead. It may concern others but it cannot deeply concern the workman. He has to look ahead to new difficulties, to wading through new times of disillusionment and weariness.

In my own place here, in the distracted crowds and in the midst of distracting things, I have often lived on little protective sayings muttered to myself. "Do not lose the fine edge of your contempt," I say to myself. Other such smart sayings come to my lips. I find myself living on them.

Of the newer men I have met you and Waldo give me something else. What friendship you give strengthens. It is a thing that cuts across the darkness and the mist.

I would not be hurt by any criticism of my efforts coming from either of you. I would like to have you both feel brotherhood for me and give me as much as you can out of your thoughts.

Is it not probably true that men like Z. lose their grip because they do not stay among workers? They cannot stand the brusqueness and hardness with which men speak who have much to do. They go among idlers where soft meaningless flattery takes the place of truth.

Well if you see things in me give me your friendship as Waldo has done. Let me see your mind at work as often as you can.

I go back to your figure of the stony field. Corn is planted there. You go about trying to cultivate, throwing stones aside. Much of the corn will be destroyed. That may be my fate. It matters so damn little.

What would matter is that one should grow into a yellow

rare ripe thing, that one should quit striving to put down roots. You get the sense of what I drive at.

Sherwood Anderson

I take the liberty of sending your note on to Frank. I will get and read the book you mention.

Chicago, Ill.,
June seventh,
Nineteen eighteen.

Dear Brooks:

If I can fix one thought in your mind I will feel more free in approaching you. When I write to men like you and Frank I do it to cut the fog of my own loneliness. If I can make you feel that no letter of mine demands answering I shall feel more freedom.

I have had an experience lately that will be of interest to you. I got suddenly an impulse to read everything I could get hold of on Lincoln. Waldo stirred up the impulse in me by giving me Charnwood's life. I read others.

I am wondering if you might not profitably go to Lincoln for a greater understanding of Twain and Whitman. There is something—a quality there—common to the three men. In Lincoln it is perhaps more out in front of you.

I got a sense of three very honest boys brought suddenly to face the complex and intricate world. There is a stare in their eyes. They are puzzled and confused. You will be inclined to think Whitman the greater man perhaps. He came closer to understanding. He lacked Lincoln's very great honesty of soul.

Twain's way lies somewhere between the roads taken by the other two men.

I am struck with the thought that I would like to have you believe that Twain's cheapness was not really a part of him. It was a thing out of the civilization in which he lived that crept in and invaded him.

Lincoln let it creep in less because he was less warm and human. He did not love and hate. In a simple solid way he stuck to abstract principles. He squares up to those principles. That's what makes him seem so big.

There is a kind of unconscious dodging in that—the country girl who died—I mean Ann—left Lincoln a thing to love that wasn't living and about. He could reach out his hand to that shadowy thing when he was lonely. It was all very fine for the making of the big stony thing that stood up sometimes before the world.

Twain got more deeply into the complex matter of living. He was more like you and me, facing more nearly our kind of problems.

Here I am going to confess something to you. Whitman does not mean as much to me as do the other two. There is somewhere a pretense about him, even trickiness. When I was a boy and another boy caught me fairly—doing some second-rate thing—I was supposed to do what we called "acknowledge the corn."

Lincoln wouldn't have done the second-rate thing.

Twain would and would have acknowledged the corn. Whitman wouldn't have owned up.

Well there you are. I am putting Whitman below where he stands in my mind.

It is unfair. It springs from a growing desire I have to sell you Twain.

Sherwood Anderson

Dear Brooks:

I have been back in the grind for two weeks now and am looking forward with joy to the notion of wiping the dust of business off my feet for at least a time. I'll come down to New York this fall and stay two or three months. I want to wander about, readjust myself, get the weariness out of me and see if I cannot face life anew.

One of the things I look forward to most is the chance of seeing more of you fellows and feeding an insistent hunger in me for companionship.

You will be amused by my memorandum of resignation to my general manager here.

Sherwood Anderson

Chicago, June 25, 1918

To: Mr. Barton
Dear Barton:

You have a man in your employ that I have thought for a long time should be fired. I refer to Sherwood Anderson. He is a fellow of a good deal of ability but for a long time I have been convinced that his heart is not in his work.

There is no question but that this man Anderson has in some ways been an ornament to our organization. His hair, for one thing, being long and mussy gives an artistic careless-ness to his personal appearance that somewhat impresses such men as Frank Lloyd Wright and Mr. Curtenius of Kala-mazoo when they come into the office.

But Anderson is not really productive. As I have said his heart is not in his work. I think he should be fired and if you will not do the job I should like permission to fire him myself.

I therefore suggest that Anderson be asked to sever his connections with the Company on August 1st. He is a nice fellow. We will let him down easy but let's can him.

Respectfully Submitted
Sherwood Anderson

New York, August 3, 1918

Dear Brooks:

Just got into town and am going into the country. I will be back here on Monday and will call you up. I want to find a hole in which to work and perhaps you can advise me. It will be good to see and talk to you.

Sherwood Anderson

Dear Brooks:

I have got settled in my own hole—427 W. 22nd St. Phone Chelsea 6140. I expect to write here every day until noon so you can reach me any morning. I have two cots so any time you will stay in town overnight I have a bed for you.

Sherwood Anderson

New York, Sept. 9, 1918

Dear Brooks:

I think I have got into a vein that may interest you and may suggest some things to your mind in connection with your thoughts of Mark Twain. I wrote a story called "The Dancer" which has nothing to do with what I have in mind. Then I began writing a story about a figure called Huey McVey, a Lincolnian type from Missouri. The story is very definite in my mind, in fact is definitely outlined. Perhaps our talk of these men led me to take one of these men up, live with him in his impulses and among his people and show if possible what influences have led him to be the kind of man we are puzzling about. I have written ten or fifteen thousand words of the tale. For the moment I have laid aside the other thing I call The Romanticist. This new tale I call The Poor White. I shall be glad to show you the outline of it. Tennessee is here and will be for two or three weeks. I want her to know you and Mrs. Brooks. Let's try to get together.

With love,
Sherwood Anderson

Owensboro, Ky.
June 24

Dear Brooks:

I have been rereading Letters & Leadership on a hot day in the Ohio River Valley and that has reminded me I have not sent on your copy of Winesburg. I will send it as soon as I get home.

My mind is a little hopeful that in Winesburg and in future novels that come from my hand you will find a real refusal to accept life on the terms it is usually presented. If that is true the result is not a conscious effort on my part but is in fact the way life has come to look to me.

The growth of that point of view is I take it what you were seeking when you wrote those remarkable papers. I do hope you will find some realization in Winesburg.

Sherwood Anderson

On train in Kentucky, Wednesday.

Dear Brooks:

Beside my own recurring thoughts of you I keep crossing your trail from time to time. The other day I went into a hospital to see the wife of a Chicago judge who is Tennessee's friend and who has been ill for a long time. She was reading your Letters and Leadership and said at once your mind had helped her understand the difficulties of American writing as nothing else had.

"I have so often not seen what you were driving at, everything you wrote seemed so incomplete. Now I see that you stand on nothing," she said. I sent her your America's Coming of Age.

In a book store I saw a Jew named Larson* who is a friend of yours. We talked of you. It was his notion you were almost too prolific, wrote too easily.

I hadn't that angle on you. "I thought he was painfully careful, almost to the point of being constipated sometimes," I said.

We discussed the matter but a few minutes. I liked the looks of him and didn't want to dispute and then I felt that

---

* Properly Max Lippit Larkin, a Russian.

he might as well as not be right and I wrong. "Everything you say shows you don't know Brooks" he declared and I took his word for it.

I have been reading The Education of Henry Adams and feel tremendously its importance as a piece of American writing. New England can scarcely go further than that. It must be in its way very complete. We do I am sure both live and die rather better in the Middle West. Nothing about us is as yet so completely and racially tired.

When you get at your Mark Twain (I suppose you already have) you must do a chapter on the American going east into that tired, thin New England atmosphere and being conquered by its feminine force.

I came West with my new book Poor White about laid by —as we out here say of the corn crop in early October. It is in shocks and stood up in the field. The husking is yet to do. I will not attempt it for a time as the proof on Winesburg should be along most any time. . . .

I am back at the old place in the advertising office. The moving picture dependence became impossible. That isn't my road out.

Back here I almost feel able to say that I don't care if I never travel again. The place between mountain and mountain I call Mid-America is my land. Good or bad it's all I'll ever have.

What I want now is to see a magazine started here in the heart of America. I want you fellows from the coast to come here. We have always been going to you. I want it changed if possible.

It isn't impossible. I will get money for the purpose. I have two or three leads that may lead to money. I shall try it out thoroughly.

Do write me the news of yourself. Give my love to Mrs. Brooks. If I were at home Tennessee would want me to wish you a happy year.

Sherwood

10th Floor, Brooks Bldg.,
Chicago

Harrodsburg, Kentucky,
Jan 8, 1919

Dear Van Wyck:

I wonder if I hurt you by my letter. I can't quite presume
to think so. It would be too absurd.

However I am writing after reading you in Sept. Dial. O,
what a relief after so much of the New York smart befuddled
writing. Those clear crisp sentences, clear crisp thoughts. It
is truly the writing Brooks I so utterly admire writing here.

Sherwood Anderson

I am still planning to hold you to your promise to read my
book.

March 31, 1919

Dear Brother Brooks:

I am so glad to hear from you that I gladly forgive you the
long silence. The winter has slipped away for me. I went
through Poor White for the first writing and then put it
away to ripen a bit. In the meantime I am doing some
experiments.

First, a new book of Tales made up of some already written
and others that are on the fire.

Second—a purely insane, experimental thing I call A New
Testament. It is an attempt to express, largely by indirection,
the purely fanciful side of a man's life, the odds and ends of
thought, the little pockets of thoughts and emotions that are
so seldom touched.

I've a fancy this last experiment would make your hair
stand on end. It is infinitely more difficult than the chants.

Why do I insist on looking upon you as the apostle of
clearness? For some reason you stand in my mind as the
supersensitive of all that is best in what is orthodox and
certain.

I am myself as uncertain as a weathercock. It seems to me that anything approaching accomplishment grows wearisome.

I want constantly to push out into experimental fields. "What can be done in prose that has not been done?" I keep asking myself.

And so I constantly set out on new roads.

What is gained—perhaps nothing but a little colorful strength in my everyday writing. I push on knowing that none will perhaps care in the least for these experiments into which I put so much emotional force.

It is at least the adventure. How I wish I could sit with you for an hour and talk of what I mean.

About Twain. I have still the hunch. Do not look too much to him for an explanation of what is not understandable in him. Think of him as a boy whipped and blown about by the winds of his times.

Look to his times, to the men and the emotions of his times. He wanted very much to be respectable. I wonder if there wasn't a touch of the inferiority complex in him. That would explain much.

He never gave himself to a great or a deep emotion, didn't dare, didn't trust himself. Whitman must have seemed a monster to him.

He stood on the doorstep of New England. It's a ridiculous notion but it's a fact. Twain with hat in hand and an apologetic air on New England's doorstep.

Good luck to you and Mrs. Brooks. I could write many pages and not say what I would like to you.

Sherwood

December 15, 1919

Dear Brother:

It is a good morning when I have letters from you and Paul, both of you have been silent so long. Well I have thought of you daily and in a way have altogether understood that your not writing was something that had nothing to do with our established feeling for each other. I am so glad about the Twain book and I do like the title. Waldo's book* came to me as an amazing, splashing, living, colorful thing. It will do something for him too, to have done this job. It will be good ground under his feet.

I put the Poor White book away when I left New York and for a long time after I came back here I was pretty much a blank dumb thing. I had you see to reestablish myself in this grim business of making a living in business. It grows constantly more like eating my own vomit.

However I have gone quite a long way with my New Testament book. I am going to print some of it in the Little Review. It is a thing without beginning or end—something that in the end I hope will express something of what you and Waldo are driving at in a semi-poetic vein.

I have up also an old book of mine called Mary Cochran which I am trying to get ready for publishing. Can't tell when it will be ready. I have little time for sustained work. How eagerly I look forward to seeing your Twain book. You will never know Brooks what your mind has meant to me, how many dark paths it has illuminated.

It is good, too, to feel that the blow that fell when Seven Arts went down did not destroy; that you, Waldo and sometimes myself too have been swimming.

Paul has his book in the publisher's hands. I had a fine letter from him today.

Waldo is out in Nebraska. There is something quiet and fine growing up in him that was always there but often out of control.

I am going to try to get to New York between Christmas and New Years for a short stay. A letter from there tells me the Dial is going to attempt being artistic and literary and is to throw politics away. Scofield Thayer and J. S. Watson, Jr. have taken over control. Stewart Mitchell is managing editor. I do not know any of them.

---

* "Our America."

Tennessee was ill for a long time but is now well and strong again. If you do come east in the Spring stop for a few days and look about here.

And give my love to Mrs. Brooks.

Write me when you can.

Sherwood

Dear Brooks:

I've been thinking about your letter of the other day and my answer that didn't say what I wanted it to say. Your not writing letters doesn't bother me. I have no special feeling about it at all.

I would in some way like you to know how I feel in another respect.

I dare say your book when it comes will not have the passionate flaming thing in it that Waldo's book often has. But Brooks you must realize what an inciter to flame in others you are.

I have a hunch you are doomed to be a man whose voice will not be heard by many here for a long time but you should realize what it means to those who do hear it.

When in speaking of Winesburg you used the word adolescence you struck more nearly than you know on the whole note of me. I am immature, will live and die immature. A quite terrible confession that would be if I did not represent so much.

I am conscious I do represent much and often I feel like a very small boy in the presence of your mind and of Waldo's too.

What is true of me is true of Sandburg, but we are different. He is submerged in adolescence. I am in it and of it but I look out. Give Sandburg a mind and you perhaps destroy him. I don't know whether that would be true of me or not.

Be sure of this Brooks. No matter how much you may seem to yourself to work in isolation it is not true. Your voice always comes clear to me and will to some others. You have been the bearer of a lamp that has illuminated many a dark place for me.

Nothing that is going to happen next year will mean as much to me as getting my hand on your new book.

You, Waldo and me—could three men be more unlike. How truly I love you two men.

Sherwood

I think of my Testament as a passionate attempt to get poetry into the thing you have expressed time and again and that you and Waldo have together made me a little conscious of. I want to have it be a distillation. God knows how far I shall succeed.

Sunday
August 24

Dear Van Wyck

A clear beautiful Sunday morning. What a stir I made within myself by writing you that letter. It was written at a time when the engine that is myself was running wildly, grinding no grain.

Someone had told me that your attitude toward my work was that it was not sound, wholesome. In myself—in my right mind—I should have paid no attention. It happened I was spiritually very tired.

There came and still come odd, hurtful reactions from some things I write—a woman I have once known—strange men and women I have never seen, write me queer abusive letters. "Why do you wallow in ugly lies about life?" they ask. I have got a dozen such letters in a week.

I put them aside—the thought of them. There were certain minds I did not expect to approve what I do. I did expect they would feel sure I was going on at my work honestly, with an intent of spiritual integrity.

You must know, must have felt how much I counted on your mind there.

The slipshod gossip that you had another attitude, joined these others in the wallowing theory would, had I not been spiritually weary, have made no impression on my mind. I did harbor it a little and am ashamed. After I had written you the letter I woke at night sick with shame. I couldn't work because of it.

I won't say I won't do the same again. When I'm tired I'm no good, a yellow dog sometimes.

As for your not knowing sometimes what I'm driving at, I don't always myself. God knows too many of my things don't fully register.

Perhaps I don't care enough. I feel myself often an instrument to adventure in flights along strange paths. Why should you ever under any circumstances feel any obligation to say anything about my work—to approve of it I mean.

A nasty, tired building up of substantiating proofs that the gossip I had heard was true must have gone on within me.

O brother Brooks please forget my silly letter.

There are lots of sweeter, finer things I can quarrel with you about at the Pittsburg meeting. I could quarrel with you indefinitely as to the value of the whole lot of political minded magazines.

I am writing a new book I'm sure you are going to love. It really does I feel get hold of a man and woman in American life intimately, intensely. Am I not a lucky dog to have this time to work undisturbed? If my damned books would only sell a little better. Is the Ordeal going to sell? I want that book to sell for other reasons than your own interest. I wish to God I could make all Americans read it.

Sherwood

Fairhope, Ala., May 15th

Dear Brother—

It was a big moment for me when I got your note and found you liked Poor White. When the novel was finished some weeks ago I said to Tennessee, "There is one man's mind

I would like to have on that book—it's Brooks." I thought of
sending it on and asking you to read it but know yours is a
busy life and hadn't the nerve. Then Huebsch did it for me
and now I have what I want. The gods are good to me. I am
also happy about two other things—that your book is at last
on the way to me and that you saw what I wanted someone
to see in the Dial story—The Triumph of the Egg. To my
mind it was one of the very best things I had ever done but
when I showed it to Paul and Waldo they did not seem much
impressed. O, Brooks, if you but knew what your own clear
fine mind has meant to me these last two or three years.
Well, there's no use trying to tell you.

It has been a wonderful time for me here these three
months. In the first place I persuaded Tennessee to be utterly
reckless, chuck her job and income and run off here with me.
That has worked out. She is getting well and is happier than
I have ever seen her. What a tremendous thing life is. For
several years she has been a tired woman. Here she rested
and then suddenly began to play. There are great quantities
of red, yellow and blue clay here—very fine and plastic—
Tennessee suddenly began working in it and already she
does really remarkable things. What new joy in life that
approach towards beauty coming in a definite form out of
herself has given her. I go about whispering to myself, "She
is going to be well. She is going to be well." O, for a world
of people not tired. What things would come out of them.

X. has been for a long time silent. Knowing nothing I still
feel I do know there is something the matter. I am sure it is
about the novel. It is not getting across with people who
have read it and away down underneath has not got across
with him but he is fighting that thought-insisting. Is my
hunch at all correct? If it is I am unspeakably sorry. I love X.
very deeply and the deep-seated desire in him to be a great
man hurts me at times like an open wound.

We will be leaving here in about a week and after that
address me at—Critchfield & Company, 10th Floor, Brooks
Bldg., Chicago. I hope to be in New York for a short stay
early in June and trust I shall see you then. There are many
things I want to talk to you about. Have begun a rollicking,

Rabelaisian book called Many Marriages, a thing I have long hungered to do. It will take marvelous good health and spirits to carry the thing off but I may never be in better shape to begin it.

Also I am painting and doing my own kind of poetry. The two things are much alike in me—mystic, vague impulses. There is a painter here who looks at my things, shakes his head and goes home and takes Epsom salts. It is perhaps the best way to take the two sides of me.

Tennessee sends love to you. Please bear our love to Mrs. Brooks. Is there any chance I may sell serial rights for Poor White to Freeman or Dial? It would give me some more freedom if I could achieve some money in this way.

With love,
Sherwood

Ephraim, Wis.—Tuesday

Dear Brooks—

This is the sort of thing that I thought might go well in the Freeman. I would not want however to sell these things at 2c per word. In a way I should rather keep them for a book I hope some day to print than to send them out at such a low price. I should be asking Dial $25 for these things. Would that be impossible for you?

Am back in the woods again and happy here. I hope to be writing pretty steadily this summer.

Sherwood

Sunday morning

Dear Brooks—

There are two reasons why Freeman can't use such things as The Man in the Brown Coat. First because it isn't any good. That reason don't go. It is. Second because Freeman is a political magazine. New Republic, Nation, Freeman. None of them give a damn for literature really. They seem to feel that creative writing has nothing to do with revolution. They want to put a new sort of government in at Washington. Well, the Freeman permits you. That's a long step.

There remains Little Review and Dial as voices for what artistic urge there may be in the country. The gods protect and nourish us. Scattered, immature, undignified, pretentious asinine things. I don't look at Little Review at all. I throw such things as Man in the Brown Coat into it.

Have just looked at the last Dial. It's spoiled eggs. Some old castrated babbler named Hueffer—or Heifer—name don't matter—a lot of other half baked stuff—no editing—no purpose—hell.

I don't know why I should swear to you about all this—most of the time I don't think about it but go on working. It did hurt though when I found you also rather taking Winesburg for example as a sex book. It got under my hide a bit. I'm usually thick skinned.

To me it seems a little as though one were permitted to talk abstractly of things, to use scientific terms regarding them—in the new dispensation—but when one attempts to dip down into the living stuff the same old formula holds. A really beautiful story like "Hands" for example is—well, nasty. God help us. Dozens of men have told me privately they knew Wing Biddlebaum. I tried to present him sympathetically—taboo.

I get so much force and reality in your Ordeal. I read it over and over like a Bible or Shakespeare's Sonnets. Twain is dead—he paid the price of caving in—but I wonder if I make you feel what I'm talking about.

In the first place I wish you could know how much I have loved—do love—your mind. I've frankly banked on it more than the mind of any other American. Am I right in my secret belief that you, down at bottom, believe me, in my reactions to life—well, not nice?* Can I—have I the privilege of caressing your mind so?

---

* No, he was wrong here. I had no such thought.—V. W. B.

I'm settled down to a quite new novel—a tale of country
life in Ohio. It has marched steadily along—a living tale I
believe full of winds and farm yards and people. I paint too
quite a lot. Your Ordeal has struck deep. It sets people talking and wondering.

Sherwood

Does Twain's formula "Freedom and the other precious
things"—still hold?

What a God damn letter. Well it's off my chest. It's glorious to have a few more months out of doors—steadily at
work.

Oxford, July 26

Dear Brooks:

I have written a note to Miss Alice Chown* and perhaps
will see her in London. We will be here all this week, then
back to London until sailing time.

The trip has been really wonderful and I for one am
bursting full of new impressions. As for Oxford—well you
know how unbelievably lovely it is. Saw Stearns in London
and he told me of the book by the American intellectual K
of Ps.** It should be quite a back breaker.

Will be in New York a few days on my way home and hope
I shall see you.

With love,
Sherwood

Dear Van Wyck:

I think also that "I'm a Fool" is a piece of work that holds
water, but do you not think its wide acceptance is largely
due to the fact that it is a story of immaturity and poses no
problem? Afer all isn't it, say, Mark Twain at his best, the
Huckleberry Finn Mark Twain?

---

* An English friend of Randolph Bourne's.—V. W. B.
** A reference to Harold Stearn's symposium, "Civilization in the United
States."

In the same book there is a story "There She Is—She is
Taking Her Bath" I would like you to read. And then the
story called "The Man Who Became a Woman" and "The
Man's Story."

One doesn't want to go on always with the childlike feeling for surface—not just that. I suppose this is my quarrel
with you—which isn't a quarrel because I love you and you
have done so much for me, cleared so many paths for me.
I mean, I presume that I do not want you to like best of my
things the things easiest to like.

I am happy that you are working again and that Paul is
working. For a long time after I came out here I was uncom-
fortable about him, feeling that he was not at work and was
disturbed for some reason. Then at last the beast wrote me
and reported himself at work and all right.

You have a kind of power over my mind, Van Wyck, of
making me think of what you are thinking and so I got
James on my mind after you got to work at him. You may
be interested to know my reactions to some solid weeks of
James reading—the feeling of him as a man who never
found anyone to love—who did not dare love. I really can't
care much for any character after he gets through with it—
he, in short, takes my love from me too.

I've a fancy—can it be true that he is the novelist of the
haters? O, the thing infinitely refined and carried far into
the field of intellectuality as skillful haters find out how to do.

It is you see but a notion but I thought it might interest
you.

I am enthusiastic about Paul's theme—"The Port of New
York"—the title is inspired.

Your garden does sound inviting. Where will I be when
I may talk now and then with the few men who give me most.

I'm working steadily on the book "Straws" and have a new
novel stirring and alive in me. I hope strongly I shall be able
to get into it this fall and winter.

My regards to Mrs. Brooks. If you get a chance please
insult Paul now and then because he does not write to me
oftener.

                                        Sherwood

33 East Liberty Street, Reno,
July

Dear Van Wyck:

I got hold of Dial with your first paper on James and it fascinated me. It was so good to find you writing again— with that clear flowing style that so got me when I first came to it.

A strange lad—that Henry—and you make one feel the strangeness and reality of him. For a time—when you were working so steadily—doing the Freeman things—I thought something in you had got pretty tired but this seems crisp and alive.

I'm sure it is going to be a fine book and only wish I could read all of it now.

Am working pretty steadily and enjoying the fact of life immensely. Last winter in New York I was tired and petulant and that has pretty much passed. I am out on the desert— plenty of sun and wind and a nice large sense of leisure.

This is another world—very distinct from the East and quite as distinct I fancy from the Pacific coast. At first the land seems dead, an endless sea of sagebrush but as you walk and ride over it the under delicacy of color, plant and flower life comes forth and sometimes—to your amazement—all flames into color.

Love and good wishes,
Sherwood

Reno, Nevada, July 30, 1923

Dear Van Wyck:

After all, Van Wyck, the danger is not imminent. The book is one that spreads out and out. I have to confine it. Get and keep it within a channel if I can.

Do I not know there has always been some of my work you do not like? But how could it be otherwise. I dare say if you and I were to see each other more closely, become really personally acquainted—which we never have quite—there would remain a difficulty.

As for myself Van Wyck—I have seen so much of ugly meaningless, drifting men that I have come to love the men I feel definitely at work and when you write me of your feeling of being crowded inside I am made happy by your letter. The feeling spreads a sense of richness, of fecundity over my consciousness of you just now and I like that.

I want to settle down really and make myself a home somewhere soon but Westport has its difficulties. Cost for one thing. You see I can live more economically any number of other places. I have to consider that.*

There are a lot of things I would like to talk with you about—the attitude of the artist, for one thing. In your Twain you come so near getting what I feel about the man but you did miss an essential thing some way.

Do you know I had, Van Wyck, a feeling that it was just the artist in Twain you in some way resented. There was somewhat the sense of a just judge trying a criminal rather than the sympathetic friend or lover.**

Can we understand at all, ever, where we do not love?

Perhaps all that struggling side of James you will feel more fully. He is more of your own world, isn't he? Twain was more of my world.

You see in my book—which after all I think I shall not call Straws—but "A Modernist Notebook"—I am frankly daring to proclaim myself the American Man.

I mean by that to take all into myself if I can, the salesmen, business men, laborers, all among whom I have lived. I do get the feeling that I, in a peculiar way and because of the accident of my position in letters, am a kind of composite essence of it all.

And actually there are days when people by thousands drift in and out of me. On a recent day here when I walked

---

* He thought for a long time of living in Westport, Connecticut, where his brother Karl had long been settled and Paul Rosenfeld and I also lived. But these were his roaming years. Karl spoke to me once of Sherwood's liking "to be alone in strange places."—V. W. B.

** He was right. It was partly the fault of my method.—V. W. B.

in the streets this natural physical feeling of being completely in rapport with every man, woman and child along a street wherein I walked became so intense that I had to go hide myself—to rest a little.

I speak of this because, when the feeling has leaked over into expression in my work you have so often said you didn't understand what I was talking about.

I want you to understand more than I can say.

And God knows I don't say this as an apology for what is not fully fruitioned in my work. No one can be more conscious of the failure of the greater part of it than I am.

But I do want you, Van Wyck, to feel for James and his difficulties, give yourself wholly to James. I can't help asking that you do it more fully than you did when you wrote of Twain.

With love,
Sherwood A.

Sunday, Reno

Dear Brooks—

When, some time ago, I asked you to take a look at this new book of mine I did not realize what a whale it was going to be. There are almost 150,000 words of it and I could not ask you to wade through any such pile. You have enough on your hands as things stand, and an unfinished book waiting. I should so much rather have you spend your time writing so that I may later read. I'll send it along to Otto Liveright who is to show it to Harpers. They may want a part of it for the magazine.

The book has you in it with many others. It contains no criticism of you but expresses the regret of a middle western workman that you seemed unwilling or unable to respond to his hunger for more intimate contact, as fellow workmen, with some of the more cultured men of the east.

As for the woman's article in Dial I did not in any way connect you with it and did not take her quotation of you as

intended to suggest you had said that particular thing of me.
I do know of course that you have been out of sympathy with
some of my work that has meant most to me and that after
some years I still think first-rate work, but I can't very well
blame you for that.

I might quarrel with such a statement as applied to Lawrence if I had you here to state at length my point of view
—which is that no man can be bogged in immaturity who
has done as much good work as Mr. Lawrence.

My dear Brooks, isn't there at least a chance that the fear
of emotional response to life may be as much a sign of immaturity as anything else? It does seem so to me.

I really think the article in Dial was ill-natured and ill-
mannered and largely made up of the fragments of ill-natured
things that have been said of me ever since I began working.
What puzzles me is the Dial. The article is so evidently in-
competent. Lord, I could have written so much sharper and
clearer criticism of myself. What the Dial is up to I can't
quite make out. They give me their praise and buy my novel
and publish it and then seem to devote themselves to a kind
of apology to the public for me.

Of course I want more than anything else freedom for you
or any other workman who really wants to work. It has been
an odd year for me. I have been more or less separated from
all the workmen I know except Stieglitz who has written me
often and some very beautiful and helpful letters this year.
Poor man, he has had a year of suffering, a part of the time
being unable to lift his arms because of pain.

I myself have had an unhappy year. I think often that a
good many people, perhaps you dear Brooks among them,
think of me as a mere reckless adventurer but I have been up
to something with my life and work. I am not a mere rudder-
less ship and now and then I do make a port.

Well, I do know that you have and always have had much
to give me and I've got some of it. I'll be glad of more. There
are not many sincere workmen in the country and in New
York in particular there is so often just a superficial slinging
of some smart saying at the head of a man, when understanding or the inclination to try to understand fails. But you

know these things as well as I do and I dare say have suffered from them as much. It is a part of the artist's life and I escape a good deal by not seeing the more ill-natured and superficial slings.

For me, anyway, work looms ahead, plenty of it. I really do begin to see a great many of my own failings and short-comings as a workman and am at least trying all the time to shake them off. And I'll be glad when I can be again where I can see and talk to men whose aims are somewhat like my own.

The book is done for better or worse and will be going off to Liveright I think some time next week.

With love,
Sherwood

Dear Van Wyck:

I am writing to ask something of you. When I have finished my "Straws," which is a kind of attempt to picture the artist in our American life, I am wondering if it would be too much trouble for you to read it.

I shall be pretty close to it and perhaps cannot judge it. It will be more or less broken and fragmentary but it is all written on a theme that has occupied your own thoughts all your life.

It is just your mind I would like on it. Will you do it?

Sherwood

The disaster would not be immediately impending.

Dear Van Wyck:

Well I shall live more like a monk after this I hope. Have got a little farm in the mountains of Virginia. We go there in the spring. Wish you could come there some time for that real getting acquainted.

Your letter only got to me after I had got back here to New Orleans. There would have been no use seeing each other in New York this trip. I saw no one—not really.

God help me I've been lecturing to help pay for the farm. Paul said he might try it. Tell him—"No."

It's no go.

I saw young Holt* and he talked of a book on me in the McBride books. I had the temerity to suggest you. It was nervy of me. He said something had been said to you and you couldn't do it.

I was glad. Had I been able to saddle you with it, would have been ashamed.

Lordy how many people are vulgar.

You find out when you go lecturing.

I hope you will really give me a chance to know you sometime.

The years fly so. There is so little done.

I am venturing a book of notes, comments, etc., this spring. I hope it may have some life in it.

Love to all in your house. We shall have a quiet house in the country soon.

Come sometime—when you want a quiet place to work—both of you.

Sherwood

I am consumed with curiosity. When shall we have a new book by you?

November 14, 1925,
Zorle, Penna.

Dear Van Wyck:

How belated I am. I have just got to your James. One reason is that the bookstores where I have been handle no books.

And what a keen delightful book this is—the same clear beautiful prose and—will you forgive my saying so—much

---

* Guy Holt.

more real sympathy with and understanding of your man than in the Twain.

The book is one I shall want to read again and again.

As ever,

Sherwood Anderson

We have bought a little farm down in Virginia and will go there to live in the Spring. New Orleans, for all its charm, is too hot for too many months. My new book seems to be selling. Now I am lecturing to pay for the farm and build a house on it. My regards to Mrs. Brooks.

S.A.

[after a long silence]

Marion, Virginia,
August Sixth,
1938

Dear Van Wyck Brooks:

I am fixing up a room in my house with framed pictures of my friends and men I admire. I spend a great deal of time alone in the country and most of you I often want to see I seldom do see. You may think it a poor substitute but a picture framed and hung up in a room I am in and out of every day does seem to bring my friends closer.

Will you please send me a picture of yourself for framing? I will be grateful.

Sincerely,
(signed) Sherwood Anderson

SA:G

Sherwood's Sweetness

by

GERTRUDE STEIN

Yes undoubtedly, Sherwood Anderson had a sweetness, and sweetness is rare. Once or twice somebody is sweet, but everything in Sherwood was made of this sweetness. Here in war-time France they have made a new sugar, grape sugar, and it is as sweet as sugar and it has all through it the tang of a grape. That was Sherwood's sweetness, it was like that.

I had a letter from him, just before he died, and when I read the letter, well it just said how do you do and how are you and glad to have heard from you, but all of it had this quality of sugar made out of grapes, it just naturally was this grape sugar substance in everything Sherwood did or was. And he was everything and he did everything.

Funny I always connect Sherwood with sweet fruits. I remember in New Orleans when he came into the room he had a bag of oranges, twenty-five for twenty-five cents, and he and we ate all the twenty-five oranges; they were orange sweet, the kind that are twenty-five oranges for twenty-five cents way are orange sweet.

Dear Sherwood, as long as grape sugar is grape sugar and it always is, and oranges twenty-five for twenty-five cents are oranges, so long will Sherwood be Sherwood. And as grape sugar will always be, and oranges will always be, so will he.

99

One cannot cry when grape sugar is like that or twenty-five oranges for twenty-five cents are like that, and one cannot die when they are like that, so one does not cry for Sherwood nor does Sherwood die.

No.

Grape sugar and oranges twenty-five for twenty-five cents, they are Sherwood.

French Reminiscence

by

Lewis Galantière

Sherwood must have had his vague notion of Paris long before he saw it, just as other men have, but the first time he mentioned it to me, it was a book that brought it to his mind. "Say," he said, "Paris must be a marvelous place. I imagine it full of great wide avenues, and palaces, and beautiful women, and then, right alongside the palaces and the avenues, streets filled with dark tenements, strangled women, men with knives, poor dirty children, thousands of simple people wondering what it's all about—and not realizing at all that they're living in a place most of us would give our eye-teeth to get to."

I admitted that that was what it was like. What could I say? It is like that.

"I've been reading about it," he went on. "I bought a book for ten cents; picked it out of a sidewalk bin in front of a second-hand bookstore. It's a wonderful story about a virtuous prostitute, and sort of about the city itself. Every morning I tear off ten pages and read them in the streetcar on the way downtown; and I throw them in the office wastebasket and tear off ten more pages the next day. I guess you must have read the book. It's called 'The Mysteries of Paris.'"

Had I read "The Mysteries of Paris!" Of course I had. But it was twenty-odd years ago that Sherwood spoke of it; and

though I was already a grown man, I was still too literary and
smug to be aware that Eugène Sue was a remarkable novelist,
a kind of French Dickens and a sociologist, an investigator
of the life of the poor, who had not his peer in France. So
I said something stupid, and we talked about other things.

Not long afterwards, Sherwood came to Paris in the company of Tennessee Mitchell and Paul Rosenfeld. It may
have been the spring of 1921. It must have been because it
was not many months after he left that he sent me a letter
to introduce a free-lance newspaper man and amateur boxer
called Hemingway, and Hemingway, I know, arrived in the
winter of '21-'22. Hemingway was a very complex and interesting fellow. I knew him intimately for about six months,
after which we drifted apart. He was very interesting, and I
often wonder what has become of him. Sherwood had a lot
of faith in him and liked him very much. I read a book he
wrote called "The Torrents of Spring" and told him he was
letting himself be influenced too much by Sherwood. Perhaps
what I said annoyed him. The book has long been forgotten,
but anyone who remembers it will know exactly what I mean.
Sherwood had a charm so potent that some people who fell
under its spell couldn't help but envy him his charm, even
while they were imitating it. But he was natural natural; and
people who are artificial natural never hit the bull's-eye the
way the natural natural do.

It isn't that there is any connection between "The Mysteries of Paris" and Sherwood's visit to Paris, except that I
pull them out of a common drawer of my memory. Sherwood's attitude to the city was the same as his attitude to the
book. Both swarmed with life, and it was true about the
palaces standing alongside the tenements. Both were filled
with light and with darkness. Both—and I think this astonished Sherwood about the city—were the domain of the little
man, and not of something silken and elegant and snobbish.
We took a train one day, Sherwood and Tennessee and Paul,
and two French friends whom I had introduced. As we were
pulling out of the Gare de l'Est Sherwood stared at the
enginemen and wipers and switchmen in the wide and dirty
yard. "You wouldn't think these little Frenchmen could do

things like running railroads, would you?" he said. He was very pleased with his remark, and chuckled.

It was on that week-end trip to Provins, I think, that he asked me if I knew Sinclair Lewis. "Well," he said, "you know, I never knew him till one day he sent me a note and asked me to lunch with him. I went to lunch. He's a nice fellow. No writer has ever said nicer things about me than he did. But he's a funny fellow, too. Kind of worried about himself because his books sell. He thinks I'm an artist, because my books don't sell; and say, that fellow wants to be an artist worse than a cow wants to have a calf!"

Sherwood wasn't backward about calling himself an artist, and it used to worry me a little, because the word was so heavy for a man so sunlit and so lacking in egocentricity. I imagine that one reason why he could use the word seriously was that he had broken his life in two at the age of forty in order to write; and if he wanted to distinguish sharply between the old life and the new, "artist" was the only word he could find to describe the new life, the new self. But it was in Paris that I saw the justification of the word.

A sensitive Frenchwoman called Marguerite Gay was translating "Winesburg, Ohio" and having trouble with certain Americanisms. "Screen door," I remember was one of them. She had never seen such a door, and the two words together bewildered her. Sherwood had written to ask me to give her a hand with her problems, and I used to go to see her at teatime. One day, as I was leaving towards seven o'clock her husband came in from his law office. She introduced me, adding in their language, "You remember, dear: this is the gentleman who is helping me with my translation of Venusbirg O-Yo." It took me a moment to understand what she was referring to.

When Sherwood came to Paris the first time in 1921, she asked him to tea. He and I walked into the room together; and as she looked at him her face went white. As soon as she was free to do it, she came over to me and whispered excitedly, "I knew he would look exactly like that! I knew it! I swear to you that, often, while working on the book or thinking about it, I have seen that man, just as he is, in my mind's eye." She was shaking all over, and as upset by her clairvoyance as if she were putting on a show for a cuckoo millionairess in Los Angeles, or for Frederick William II of Prussia, the libertine lover of table-tipping.

Now what I conclude from this true tale is that you don't have visions of favorite authors as people of ordinary looks and natures. The man Mme. Gay "saw" must be describable as an artist; and since Sherwood was the spit and image of the man she "saw" . . . Q.E.D.

But about this there can be no question anyway. If he hadn't written a line, Sherwood was still an artist. You had only to hear him tell a story, to watch him as, sitting characteristically on the end of his chair, both elbows planted on the table, his chin in the air and cigarette loosely held in his curved right hand, he spun out his tale, paused, looked down, wiped an imaginary crumb off the table with the flat of his hand, looked suddenly up and went on with the story, to know that here was a man who put shape, design, into whatever he did. (Read "Death in the Woods" and you'll see what I mean.) And the life in those stories was something that opened your mouth with delight, though the story might be about his homonymous neighbor, Mrs. Anderson the mountain woman, or the butcher in Marion, or a Chicago advertising man. And his voice was the most American voice that I can imagine. It wasn't rural in the sense of the stage comic, but rural in the impression it gave of a man of the frontier. It was just the voice that was missing from an otherwise admirable production of "Abe Lincoln in Illinois." I don't say that people round Springfield in the 1840's and 1850's spoke as Sherwood did; I say that if Sherwood had spoken Lincoln's lines the audience would have believed it was listening to a voice out of that age and off that frontier.

I said that we had taken a train one day to Provins. Provins is one of those towns you come upon by chance and actually succeed in getting back to. It is not picturesque, and you don't exhaust it in a visit as you do Carcassonne. A thousand years ago it was the seat of the counts of Brie and Champagne and one of the great market towns of Europe. One of the most celebrated of all troubadours, Thibault of Champagne, reigned, sang, and minted the coin of his own realm there. In 1921 it was still a solid market town, filled on Saturdays with the farm population of the surrounding country. The Boule d'Or, where we stayed, was in the "new" town which dated from the fourteenth century and lay in the valley. Thibault had reigned from the "old" town on the top of the hill, where stood the ancient grange, now a museum, with its Roman sarcophagi, the flat village square flanked by the squat stone houses and overshadowed by the donjon called Caesar's Tower which had had a French king for prisoner, and surrounded by the still magnificent wall in which the British had made a breach in the time of Joan of Arc and near which stood a farmhouse that had been the headquarters of a British Army Corps in 1915.

Off the square in the "old" town was a café, and behind the café a small trellised arbor. We had drinks there, and we talked, and Sherwood read some verse he'd written down in a notebook that he carried in his pocket. I don't remember the verse but I remember the voice—grave and sweet and marked by that particular accent he had ("neither" was *nother* and "either" was pronounced like *other*). I don't mean that it was a solemn session. We were sitting at a table, and we were smoking and drinking vermouth, or some such drink; and we were chatting and laughing and pointing out to one another the beauty of the prospect and the peace of the place. But in and out, the poems wove through our talk, the voice of Sherwood glided through it, and I saw suddenly that an old woman, her back really bowed down as if in a movie, stood at one end of the arbor, listening to words she could not understand. I spoke to her, and she said, *"Je ne sais pas ce qu'il dit, ce monsieur, mais il me plaît."* I told Sherwood that she said she liked him, even though she couldn't understand him, and he looked at her and laughed his friendly laugh.

"Couldn't we get a bite to eat here?" he suggested suddenly. It was about six in the evening. They said no, they never served food, had none except to feed themselves. I said something about an omelette being easy to make, a tin of sardines easy to open; but they were stubborn until Sherwood smiled at the old woman. *"Oh, oui,"* he said. *"Une omelette, qu'est-ce que c'est, une omelette?"* And he added, "Why, c'est nothing at all!" He got the omelette, got the sardines, got, I remember, some cold ham. And all this we found ready for us on the table in the arbor after a tour of the fruit and vegetable garden in which, walking beside Sherwood and not quite daring to take his arm, the old lady had shown him every plot and shown him, too, the espaliers of pears that grew along the garden wall.

Sherwood was happy in France, and the reason was somewhat that the French liked him so much. He was like Voltaire's Huron to them—not a Ph.D. who spoke their language correctly [which they would naively take for granted], and knew the difference between Maurice Scève and Louise Laké [which would not interest them]. He carried with him, wherever he went, the authentic American culture, and he made America appear to be what at its best it is—a band of shrewd, friendly, unenvious, goodlooking people; not particularly concerned to understand other men, but ready to appreciate them and very far from assuming that there wasn't room in the world for their kind and his too. Had he lived, and had Nelson Rockefeller's committee possessed discernment, Sherwood might have been the perfect Yankee apostle to the Latin Americans. There never was an American who had a sweeter touch for other men than Sherwood had.

A Letter from Thomas Wolfe

DEAR SHERWOOD:

Thanks for your letter. It was not only fine to hear from you—what you said did me a lot of good. What you say is true—I do, and have all of my life gone for everything—not only writing—hell for leather. I seem to wrestle with each experience as if, in circus talk, I am "now about to engage in a hair-raising, spine-freezing, gravity-defying duel to the death with the universe." I suppose that's why that shrewd and wise and nice mother-in-law of yours told you I was pretty hard on myself. I went home this summer for the first time in about eight years to fight it out, talk it out, live it out with the city of Asheville as if I was a regiment of storm troops going into a decisive battle. And of course it took it out of me. I was pretty tired when I saw you—but maybe also, I was coming away with a lot of tar on my heel and large potfuls of the nature earth. I hope so, anyway. I didn't think really I'm so much worried about the talk of flood of my writing as I ever was. I've got a feeling about some things, after long mulling at thinking about and with them that often turns out right—and my feeling is that I shall probably always have to do essentially about as I do now— that is, pour it out, boil it out, flood it out. I realize myself through a process of tonatial production. Perhaps there are

107

*better ways but that is my way—I believe essentially my way
—and it would be wrong to worry a lot—doing it Flaubert's
way, or Hemingway's way, or Henry James' way. Nevertheless, I do worry, as we all do, about my improvement—I want
to be a better writer, a less wasteful writer, a sincere writer,
a clever writer, a more disciplined writer—and I believe and
hope that may come through work. As to the rest of it, my
death-defying duel with the universe—just the business of
living which I make so damned hard, but out of which I do
believe I have managed to get a good deal—I think it is pretty
closely hooked up with my work. In fact, living and working
are so close together with me that it seems to me they are
damned near the same thing. I do carry my work too much
with me—when I'm doing it, I take it into bars, restaurants,
railroad trains, parties, upon the streets everywhere. I guess
many a row or quarrel or dispute in some joint with a sanded
floor began somewhere hours or days or weeks before upon a
page of mss., but I hope some of my better moments started
there as well.*

*I'm usually with a large burden of work—three monstrous
books, all worked upon and sweat upon and prayed about and
cursed upon for years—I'm caught in the Loacoon (sic) coils
of this too-muchness. I get maddened like Tantalus with the
feeling of being everything about nothing, my group, and of
clinging to death. I think I am starving for publication: I love
to get published; it maddens me not to get published. I feel
at times like getting every publisher in the world by the scruff
of his neck, forcing his jaws open, and cramming the mss.
down his throat—"God-damn you, here it is—I will and
must be published."*

*You know what it means—you're a writer and you under-
stand it. It's not just "the satisfaction of being published."
Great God! it's the satisfaction of getting it out, of having
that, so far as you're concerned, gone through with it; that
good or ill, for better or for worse, it's over, done with, finished, out of your life forever and that, come what may, you
can at least, as far as this thing is concerned, get the merciful
damned easement of oblivion and forgetfulness.*

Really, I don't think I'm either muddled or confused. I

don't think I know anyone who knows, or thinks he knows, so clearly and so desperately what he wants to do.

I want to do my work and to get it published. I want to find a place where I can feel at home and to which I can go back (incidentally, I think there are such places, but I don't think they're either Asheville or New York). I want to get married and try to have a family.

I'll probably always go through this kind of struggle with my work, but honestly I don't see why I shouldn't get all these things I have spoken of. At any rate I shan't give up trying yet.

May I also say that I want to be your friend, as I am, and I want you to be mine, as I believe you are. When I told you how I felt about you and your work, I was not laying it on with a trowel; I don't think of you as a father, as an elderly influence, or anything of the kind. So far as I know, your work has not "influenced" me at all, sure in the ways in which it has enriched my life, and my knowledge of my country. I think you are one of the most important writers of this century, that you plowed another deep furrow in the American earth, revealed to us another beauty that we knew was there but that no one else had spoken. I think of you with Whitman and with Twain—that is, with men who have seen America with a poet's vision and with a poetic vision of life, which to my mind is the only way ultimately it can be seen.

I appreciate your letter, and all you say to me. I'll have to work the whole thing out for myself, but I feel there is wisdom in you, and we never perhaps give up the wonderful urge of our youth that we will find someone, external to our life and superior to our need, who knows the answer.

It does not happen—"is not my strength in me?"—but it comes, I think, from the deepest need in life, and all religiousness is in it.

Good-bye for the present, Sherwood, I hope I'll be here when you come. At any rate, I'll look forward to seeing you again before too long. Meanwhile, with love to all,

Yours

TOM WOLFE.

The above letter written by Thomas Wolfe to Sherwood Anderson, September 22, 1937, is printed by the kind permission of Thomas Wolfe's executor, Maxwell Perkins, editor of Scribner's, and Wolfe's editor and mentor during his life.

Anderson The Storyteller

by

HENRY MILLER

I MUST SAY, to begin with, that I hardly knew Sherwood Anderson the man, having met him only in the last year of his life and then only two or three times. I had always lived in the hope of meeting him one day because I was extremely curious to observe whether he could tell a story as well as he could write one. My admiration for his tales has been and always will be unbounded. Only a couple of months before our accidental meeting, in the lobby of his hotel, I had made an impromptu speech about him before a group of Greek friends in Constitutional Square, Athens. I remember well how pleased he was when I requested him to affix his signature to a few of his volumes which I was sending to my Greek friends shortly after my return to America. I was even more pleased than he because the volume which I prized most— "Many Marriages"—was being dispatched to one of the greatest storytellers I have ever met, George Katsimbalis of Amaroussion, whom I have written about in "The Colossus of Maroussi."

The good fortune I have had to know a few remarkable storytellers is due, I suppose, to the fact that I am what is called "the perfect listener." The ones I admire most, not forgetting the great Katsimbalis, are Hans Reichel, the

111

painter; Blaise Cendrars, a French author known only
slightly to American readers, more's the pity; and Conrad
Moricand of Paris, an astrologer and occultist. Had I become
better acquainted with Anderson there is no telling where
I might place him in the rank of fascinating raconteurs. But
I have only the memory of several all too brief meetings, and
these in the presence of other persons.

This epitaph which is now being written by his friends
and admirers reminds me sadly of the posthumous homage
paid to Elie Faure in the pages of "L'Europe" shortly after
Faure's death. It seemed incredible to me at the time that a
great artist such as Faure should have been so neglected in
a country like France where writers and painters have been
esteemed even by the common people. There was an unde-
niable feeling, in the case of Faure, that his prose might not
be good French prose, whatever that is supposed to mean. In
the case of Anderson there has also been a question, I believe,
about the validity of his distinctly personal style of writing.
Yet in both cases, though the two are vastly dissimilar in style
and genius, we have undoubtable evidence of an eloquence
which is not only rare but moving and profound. Anderson,
it seems to me, was always trying to ferret out the artist—
even in the poorest soul. I think that in an unconscious way
he was trying to demonstrate the universality of art and the
ubiquity of the artist even in a country like ours where the
artist is despised and treated like a dog.

I suppose the remark he made upon the occasion of our
very first meeting is one that all his friends are familiar with.
I had the feeling that he must have said it over and over
again. It was a sort of apology to the effect that he had really
stolen his material from other men—not from other writers,
to be sure, but from simple, unsuspecting people who had no
realization of the artistic possibilities hidden in their crude,
faltering tales, the tales he listened to so patiently and rev-
erently. The way he put it rather surprised me for I had
always been of the opinion that the writer looked to life for his
material and not to his own empty little head. But Anderson,
stressing it the way he did, laughing a bit sheepishly as he
spoke, was either suffering from a guilt which was absurd or

else revealing his abnormal sense of honesty. Perhaps too
there was something artful about his naiveté, a desire possibly
to disguise the amount of labor he put into the telling of his
artless tales. All the superb writers of stories, those especially
who have a weakness for simplicity, slave like convicts over
their manuscripts. Integrity and respect for one's métier are
not the only explanations of this passionate, self-imposed toil.
Writers of this genre get their material directly from life.
Being artists, they are not content with the imperfections of
life but seek to refine the crude ore to bare, abstract quintes-
sentials. They strive to make life more lifelike, as it were. It
is a dilemma which will never be straddled by craftsmanship.
The better their stories become the worse for art. Art and life
are separate and the only link between them is the artist himself who, as he reveals himself more and more, realizes that
union between the two which is entirely a matter of creation.
Entirely a question of daring, I might say, for what is creation
but imagination made manifest? The scrupulousness and
meticulousness of the simplifier is a sign of fear. The nature
or content of the story is nothing; the approach, the handling
of it is everything. Saroyan is today the most daring of all our
storytellers and yet I feel that he is timid. He is timid, I mean,
judged by his own criteria. His evolution is not in the direction one would imagine. He took a big hurdle in the beginning, but he refuses to go on hurdling. He is running now
and his stride is pleasant and easy, but we had expected him
to be a chamois and not a yearling.

   Of the storytellers I have known the best are those who
tell them. In the case of those who do both I prefer the man,
the natural storyteller, to the writer. In saying this I feel I
am paying these men a greater tribute than if it were the
other way round. A story, to achieve it full effect, must be
told; there must be gestures, pauses, false starts, confusion,
raveling and unraveling, entanglement and disentanglement.
There ought to be a certain amount of self-consciousness and
embarrassment followed by a complete forgetfulness of self,
followed by ecstasy and abandon and delirium. A story
should be written in the air, consigned to the four winds,
forgotten the moment it is told. In itself it is nothing—an act

of creation of which there are millions taking place constantly. The only important thing about a story is that a man felt like telling it. To preserve it between cloth covers and study it as if it were a dead insect, to try and imitate it or rival it or surpass it, all this is lost motion and kills creation. The storyteller is an actor who enriches and enhances the sense of life. The writer of short stories is more often than not a pest. If he is not doing it to keep a wife and child from starvation he is doing it because he was defeated in his original aims, whatever they may have been. The writers of short stories, as a rule, do not go about their work joyously, recklessly, defiantly; they go at it grumblingly, grudgingly, with the most silly, painstaking effort, one eye on the clock and the other on the imaginary and often invisible pay check. They give their life blood to make it easy for uncreative dolts to pass the time away. The reward, when or if it comes, only serves to embitter them. They do not have an audience— they have "customers" who desert them like rats the moment a more tempting piece of cheese is dangled before their eyes.

What impressed me about Anderson was his genius for seizing on the trivial and making it important and universal. A story like "The Triumph of the Egg" is a classic. (In one of his latest books, "Kit Brandon," there is another magnificent achievement, a little story in itself about the man who became a horse, who got down on all fours and *was* a horse for ten or fifteen minutes—such a horse as was never seen on land or sea or in the sky or in the myth.) I was extremely happy to be able to tell Anderson how much I enjoyed that book, "The Triumph of the Egg." It fell into my hands at a time when, in complete despair over my inability to say what I wanted to say, I was about to give up. That book encouraged me. All Anderson's books did. (Up to "Dark Laughter," when I practically ceased reading American authors.) He seemed to have the real, the authentic American voice. The style was as free and natural, I thought then, as the glass of ice water which stands on every table in every home and restaurant. Later I learned that it was not so free and natural, that it had been acquired through long apprenticeship.

In Anderson, when all is said and done, it is the strong human quality which draws one to him and leads one to prefer him sometimes to those who are undeniably superior to him as artists. This quality I felt immediately when I met him. Dos Passos, whom I had also just met for the first time, was with us. We repaired to a bar nearby, just the three of us. "Now talk!" I said to myself. "Prove to me that you are the born storyteller I have always believed you to be!" And he did. That quality which I adore so much, that mania for trivia (which Cendrars has to an even greater degree) came immediately to the fore. I clung to every word he dropped, as though they were little round nuggets of gold. His way of stringing the words together, of breaking off, of fumbling and faltering, of searching and stumbling, all this was exactly as I had experienced it in his writing.

This talk of his, so natural, so easy-flowing, so gentle and good-humored, welled out of a man who was in love with the world. There was no malice, no chagrin, no meanness or pettiness about his language. At the worst there was a quiet melancholy—never a feeling of disillusionment. He had an unbounded faith in the little man. I think myself he made too much of him, but that is rather in Anderson's favor. One can't make too much of the nonentities; they are the hope of the future.

Other writers whom I have met were very much like their books. Anderson was more than his books. He was all his stories plus the man who wrote them—plus the man who *listened* to them! You could tell from the way he told a story about some character he had met, some trivial incident which had stuck in his crop, that he had a reverence for his material which was almost religious. He didn't try to dominate or control or direct his subject matter. He always let his man speak for himself. He had the patience not just of the artist but of the religious man: he knew that there was bright shining ore beneath the scabby crust. He knew that fundamentally everything is of equal value, that manure is just as vital and inspiring as stars and planets. He knew his own limitations too. He didn't write about the common man as though he were some rare bird just discovered by the sociologist or his caricature the social worker; he wrote about the common man because he was one himself and because he could only write about men and women he knew and understood.

I was told by one of his friends that when Anderson arrived in Paris and saw for the first time the Louvre, the Seine, the Jardin des Tuileries, he broke down and wept. The story has an authentic ring. Anderson had the gift of surrender. He was humble and reverent. He could become ecstatic about a knife and fork. He also recognized and admitted his own weaknesses—could make fun of them when it suited him to do so. He didn't try to crowd his fellow-artists off the map; all he asked was that they make a little space for him, permit him to be one of them, one of the least among them. Sterling qualities and so rare nowadays.

Stressing the storyteller, as I do, I want to make a distinction, a very vital one, between him and the professional storytellers with whom America is infested. The professional storyteller bores me to tears. His yarns are sterile, saddening and maddening. What one misses in them is creation. All that they seem to accomplish, all indeed that they aim to accomplish obviously, is to postpone that moment which the American dreads most, the moment when he will be alone with himself and know that he is empty.

The other kind of storyteller, such as Anderson, is never trying to stave off a vacuum. If he tells a story it is to create a mood, an atmosphere, in which all may participate. He isn't seeking to hold the floor or put himself in the spotlight. He isn't worried about awkward silences or whether the evening will be a success or not. It's an exchange, a communion through words, by means of which the unique experiences of the others present may be melted into the common fund of human experience and make of a simple gathering a feast of real brotherliness. I liked the very way in which Anderson sat down to the table on the several occasions we were together. He plunked himself down to stay, secure in the knowledge that if nobody else had anything to contribute *he* did, because he never came without his instrument, I mean that instrument which he had made of himself. *He brought himself along*, that's how I want to put it. *And he gave himself!* What a relief to encounter such a man! Naturally his stories were good. They were like ripe fruit dropping from an overladen tree. You wouldn't want a man like that to argue with you, as Americans seem determined to do whenever they come together. You wanted to listen, to dream, to wander off in your own mind just as he wandered off in his. You felt that you had his silent consent to do as you pleased. He wasn't fastening you down with a beady eye or expecting you to smile at the right moment or applaud him when he got through. He didn't pretend to be the Almighty telling the story of Creation. He was just an interpreter, a mouthpiece, an actor doing his part. You felt easy and rested when he had finished his story. You knew that another was coming if you'd just give him time to finish his drink or wipe his mouth. He made you feel that there was all the time in the world, that there was nothing better to do than doing just what you were. Part of him wasn't off somewhere trying to catch a train or organize a strike. He was all there and giving of himself in his easy, steady way ("easy does it!"), giving what was ripe and ready to fall to the ground, not straining, not pumping it up, not wondering if it were just the right quality or not.

And that's how I like to think of him now that he's gone. I like to think of him as a quiet, easy spirit seated at a round table under a shady tree holding converse with other departed spirits. Probably talking about celestial trivia, the stuff that wings are made of, or some such thing. Drinking celestial ambrosia and comparing it with the earthly imitations. Feeling the ethereal grass or stroking the astral cows. "A beautiful place!" I can hear him saying. "Rather like I imagined it would be. Not so different from down below either." Yes, I can follow him as he strolls leisurely about looking for a bridge perhaps where there might be a contented fisherman, wondering to himself what the man's story might be. Thanking his stars, no doubt, that here at least he will not be expected to put it down on paper. An eternity in which to wander about, touching things, smelling things, and swapping stories with old and new comers.

Most people think of Heaven as a boring place, but that's because they are themselves bores. I'm sure Anderson isn't finding it boring. Heaven was just made for him. And when we get there some day and meet him again what heavenly stories he'll have to beguile us with!

I don't feel the least bad about his passing. I envy him. I know he's at peace there, as he was here.

His Collaborators

by

WILLIAM SAROYAN

I HAVE ALWAYS remembered how wonderful I felt when I read about the cabbages which were thrown against the door of the house where he lived, as though that house and the people in the house were an act of vaudeville no one could understand; and how sweet it was that his mother gathered the cabbages and cooked them for the family. Now, now that he is dead, it seems a little clumsy to be wanting to thank him for the story of the father and the egg—the egg which triumphed; the story which came along on the great page of writing and said to each of us, The nearest wall is where you'll find the writing; the area closest is the place; the people there are the heroes.

His writing made you say, I can do that. (And many of us did. We said it and we did it, each of us bringing the little more, or the little less, that we could not help bringing.) We were his collaborators who did not need to talk things over first. He set up a school whose doorway was anywhere we happened to be, and we all walked in and out whenever we pleased. Sometimes he was so simple we had to say, I can do *better* than that. Now and then we became scoundrels and said of what he said, it is too soft, too tender, too much the same—what the hell does he think he is looking for—something? And we meant that he was only searching, but not for

119

anything; at least not anything that was not plain and even a little childish. He walked around it, came close to it, went away, returned, but he never wanted to take it over or look at it sharply—he wanted to pretend that it was really what he wanted it to be—wonderful. But if he was a simpleton, we had better remember it; we had better appreciate it; and we had better not imagine that it would have been the same had he been an authority on political science, for instance. His story—the story he wrote—is a lonely story; it is the story of the stranger in the streets. It is shot through with a solemn silence; and yet there is no peace in it; he never decided that it was all a little foolish, everywhere, or that there could be another way to make it endurable. His way was to insist upon its wonder. I remember reading in *Vanity Fair* about a visit he made to Hollywood, but he was the same there as any-where else. He found nothing laughable about the place or his being there. He was restless and eager anywhere. In a way he was the only living American writer, but I can't figure out why it took him so long to get started or why he stopped so easily, after beginning. The beginning he made was so right; it was almost American writing's beginning.

When I was twenty or so I heard him give a lecture in Los Angeles and I have never forgiven him for that. What he said was ridiculous. He didn't look right, either. He looked soft. The tone of the talk was wrong. He was squawking. It wasn't angry, it was nagging. He seemed to feel that Ameri-can life was not what it should be, and he mentioned people as though they had failed him—as though it had been a deliberate plot to embarrass *him*. I got into the lecture free, with a reporter; the reporter wanted to interview him and asked if I wanted to go along. I didn't.

I read one of his short stories in the Pocket Books collection of American short stories a couple of days ago. It wasn't right, but it wasn't one of his good stories. There was a lot of stuff in the story that made you feel maybe he was never much, which is no way to feel about this writer, because in his better stories he was the best.

His dying, like his writing, lacked impact, and I feel like a dog saying this. He told us many good things. He made it possible for us to sit down and write. He introduced us to our world and to one another.

But forget all this stuff—if his dying lacked impact, and if I am so smart I can find fault with his work, why did I feel so miserable when I read that he was dead?

The Champion

by

JESSE STUART

I count it a special favor that you are doing me by asking me to contribute to this memorial number for Sherwood Anderson. Sherwood Anderson liked the unusual characters among men. He wrote these stories with a language that was almost Biblical simplicity. I am sending you a very brief story about a man swallowing corn with a rooster. This is unbelievable, but there is a fine-looking boy in our country today with a ruined stomach over trying to swallow more corn than a rooster. He is my brother's wife's first cousin. So I am sending this along. I believe that Sherwood Anderson would like this story if he were a living man at this hour and could read it.

"Now Lester you know that I can outeat you," Sam White-apple said as he followed me down the path from our house to the barn. "I ain't seen anybody yet that I can't outeat."

Sam stood in the path and looked me over. He slapped his big stummick with his big pitchfork hands. He had walked six miles to get me to try to outeat him.

"Right here's where I put the grub," he said. "This old nail keg will hold it."

Sam laughed a big horse laugh and showed two rows of yaller teeth. His beady, black eyes squinted when he looked into my eyes. Sam looked tough as a shelled-bark hickory too.

His face was covered with black beard—so black that it made his yaller teeth look like two white rows of corn between his beardy lips. Sam was a hardworkin' man, too, fer his overall knees were threadbare and the seat of his overalls was good as new. His overall suspenders had faded on his blue work-shirt. His gray-checked cap bill stood over his face like a front porch.

"I've heard you was a great eater," Sam said. "I've just come over to put you under the table. I want to show you who is the champion eater in these parts."

"It's in crop time Sam," I said. "Any other time but now."

"Why not now?" Sam ast.

"It knocks me out," I said. "I don't want to be knocked out. I've got too much work to do."

"You know which side of your bread is buttered," Sam laughed. He bent over until he nearly touched the ground, he slapped his ragged overall knees, and laughed. "Old Bean-pole Lester Pratt can't take it. You got a mouth big enough to shovel in grub, but you can't take it. The eatin' champion-ship goes to Raccoon Creek. There's where I winned it from Gnat Hornbuckle when I et a hog's head."

"That ain't no eatin'," I said. "I could eat that much and still be hungry."

"What about five stewed hens and all the trimmings?" Sam said. "I winned the chicken eatin' contest over on Uling Branch. I was full to the neck. Didn't think I could get the last bite down my gullet but I did."

"You didn't eat that many hens."

"Ast Porky Sturgill," Sam said. "He et the least—just a couple of hens. He had to pay for all the hens six men et. I'll tell you it's fun to get a real square meal and let the other feller pay fer it. I've never paid fer a meal yet. I've winned every eatin' contest. I've got the nail keg to put it in and you've just got a hollow beanpole there."

Sam hit me on the stummick and laughed as I started to open the barnlot gate.

"Wonder if Sam could outeat a cow," I thought. No, he couldn't eat corn nubbins, fodder or hay. Wonder if he could outeat a mule. No, a mule et more roughness than anything else. Sam couldn't eat hay or fodder. Then it flashed through my mind if Sam could outeat a hog. But Sam couldn't eat the things a hog et. Sam wouldn't get down and drink slop from a trough and gnaw corn from the cob on the ground. What could he eat with?"

Just then my black game rooster run across the barnlot. He could always put away more corn than any chicken I'd ever seen. He'd eat so much corn I often wondered where he put it. He was tall with a long neck and a big craw. His face was red as a sliced beet. He didn't have any comb for it was cut off so other roosters couldn't peck it when I took him to fight.

"Sam you're braggin' about your big nail-keg stummick," I said. "You can't eat as much shelled corn as that rooster."

"You wouldn't try to be funny would you?" Sam ast.

"No, I mean it."

"Huh, never et with a rooster but I'd just like to show you," Sam said. "If I could eat the same grub, I'd eat with a mule, horse, cow or hog. It wouldn't make no difference to me. I've fed livestock around the barn and I know how much they eat. I know how much I can eat. I'll tell you I've got a big capacity. When I drink water in the cornfield it takes a gallon bucket full of cold water to make me a swig. You talk about that little chicken! You make me laugh."

The rooster stopped in the barnlot. He held his head up to one side and cackled. He looked at us with the glassy-lookin' eye that was turned toward us. His red face beamed. It wasn't as large as the side of a big watch. I looked at the rooster and then I looked at Sam. He stood head and shoulders above me. I didn't know he was so tall. He looked short for his shoulders were so broad and his stummick bulged out so in front. His sleeveless arms looked like fence posts folded across the bibs of his overalls. Sam was bigger than a lot of fattenin' hogs I'd seen. Maybe he could outeat my tall slim game rooster; I didn't know. But if he did, he would have to put a lot of corn in his craw!

"Can old Sam outeat you boy?" I ast my rooster.

My black game rooster cackled. He cocked his head to one side and looked at Sam. He cackled louder.

"He says that you can't outeat him, Sam," I told Sam.

"Said he was ready to take you on!"

"That rooster can't understand what you say," Sam laughed. He looked at me as if he believed though that the rooster could understand what I said.

"Can he outeat you boy?" I ast my rooster.

He cackled louder than ever. He cackled like he was skeered.

"W'y that silly chicken," Sam chuckled. "You shell the corn and I'll show you whose the champion of this barnlot in just a few minutes. I won't haf to swaller enough corn to spile my dinner to beat him."

We walked from the gate down to the corncrib. The chickens followed me to the crib for I allus shelled 'em corn in front of the crib. The rooster walked toward us cacklin' like he was tryin' to say somethin'.

"What's your rooster sayin' now?" Sam ast.

"He's cussin' you," I said. "He says that you can't eat corn with a chicken."

"Tell him in chicken talk that I got a good gullet," Sam said. "Tell him I got a place to put shelled corn that's bigger than his craw."

I opened the crib door and got a ear of corn. I shooed the rest of the chickens back from the crib. My rooster stood there. He wouldn't shoo. He wasn't a chicken that you could shoo easily. If you shooed him too much he was liable to fly at your face and try to spur you. He never had as much as he could eat for I left 'im in fighten' trim. Now I would give him all that he could eat. He stood with his neck feathers ruffled up like he was goin' to fight. His feathers were black and shiney as a crow's wing. His spurs were straight as sourwood sprouts and sharp as locust thorns. He acted like he owned the barnlot and that he would as soon spur Sam as to outeat him.

"Now Sam I'll give him a grain of corn everytime I give you one," I said.

"Any old way suits me," Sam said. "This eatin' contest aint going to last long nohow. I'm just doin' this fer fun to say that I outet Lester Pratt's black game rooster since old Beanpole Lester was afraid to eat with me."

Sam ketched the grain of corn in his big mouth when I pitched it to him. It was fun fer Sam. He laughed and swallered the corn. Then I pitched my rooster a grain. He picked it up in his hooked bill and swallored it. He quirked and wanted more.

"He laughed at you Sam," I said.

"Throw us the corn," Sam said. "We'll see who laughs last."

Sam stood there a big giant in our barnlot. I'd throw a grain of corn first to Sam and then one to my rooster. The hens stood back. They were wantin' the corn that I was throwin' to Sam and to my rooster but Sam thought they were lookin' on and hopin' that their hero would win.

That ear of corn didn't last as long as frost on a hot plate. I kept shellin' corn and pitchin' to Sam and my rooster until my arm got tired. Every time a hen quirked or made a funny noise in her throat Sam thought she was makin' fun of him. He would screw up his big beardy face and look sour at something little as a hen. Sam stood by the corncrib. He never moved out of his tracks. He would stand there and crane his big bull neck and swallow.

"Aint your throat gettin' awful dry,?" I ast.

"Nope, it aint," Sam said. "A little grain of corn just draps down my gullet. You'd better ast your rooster and see if his throat is gettin' dry."

Just then I pitched my rooster a grain of corn and he sneezed.

"My rooster says his throat is okay," I said.

Sam looked a little funny when the rooster sneezed. I could tell he didn't have the confidence that he did have when we started the contest. Sam was lookin' a little worried. Maybe it was because of all the noises the chickens made.

"Am I 'lowed to chew my corn?" Sam ast.

"Nope you're not," I said. "The rooster aint got no teeth and you're supposed to swaller your corn like he does. What's a little grain of corn nohow?"

"Nothin' to look at it," Sam groaned, "but a lot of swallowed corn gets heavy. I can feel a heavy lump right down at the end of my gullet."

"I guess my rooster feels it too," I said. "Watch him stretch his neck when he swallers a grain."

I looked down at my feet and there was a pile of corncobs big enough to start a fire in the fireplace. There was a pile of cobs big enough to cook a big dinner in our cookstove. I'll tell you it was horse and cat between Sam and my rooster. At first I thought Sam would swallow more corn than my game rooster. Now I doubted that he would. I wondered where my rooster was puttin' so much corn. His craw had begun to swell. When he reached down to get a grain he nearly toppled over from the weight of his craw. But he reached down and picked up a grain, stood up as straight as Sam, and swallowed it.

"I'd like to have a sip of water," Sam said. "I'd like to dampen my gullet. It's gettin' a little dry."

"My rooster aint ast fer water yet," I said. "You've got to abide by the same rule he does. See he's never made a sound. He just stands up straight and swallers his corn."

"It's gettin' hard to get down," Sam said as he craned his neck and twisted his head from first one side to the other.

I could see now that Sam was worried. His eyes showed it. He didn't have any confidence at all. My rooster looked cheerful. He acted that way when he picked up a grain of corn in his fightin' beak. His eyes looked bright. He was confident and in fine spirits.

"Where's that chicken puttin' all that corn?" Sam ast.

"I don't know," I said. "You will haf to ast the chicken."

But Sam Whiteapple didn't ast the chicken. Old Sam kept strugglin' with a grain of corn. He was tryin' to get it down. His eyes begin to look watery. And Sam didn't have his natural color. There was a place on Sam's cheek where the beard didn't reach and that was allus rosy-red. Now it was turning pale. Sam moved out of his tracks when he tried to get another grain down. He run a little circle like a dog followin' his tail when he lays down. I kept my eye on Sam to see that he didn't spit the grain of corn out. Finally Sam got it down. My rooster swallowed his but he acted like he was gettin' plum full up to his ears. His craw was swellin' all the time. But 'peared like he knowed what was up. And he was goin' to beat Sam.

I pitched Sam another grain of corn. He ketched it in his big mouth. I never saw a big man wrestle with a little grain of corn like Sam did. He worked and worked and finally he got it down by screwin' up his face, gruntin' and groanin' and runnin' a little circle. Tears come to his eyes and flowed down his beardy cheeks.

" 'Pears like I got a bushel of shelled corn in my gullet," Sam said. "It's lodgin' now in my windpipe. I'm gettin' short of breath."

I had just pitched my rooster another grain of corn and he had had time to grab it when Sam fell like a tree. If my rooster hadn't been a quick one, he wouldn't 've got out of Sam's way. Sam sprawled like a sawed-down oak on the barnlot. His arms fell limber as two rags. It skeered me nearly to death. I shook Sam. He wouldn't talk. He didn't move or anything. His mouth was open and I saw three grains of corn on his tongue. I felt to see if his ticker was still goin'. I thanked my God that it was. My rooster walked away with his flock of hens. He was craw-heavy for he almost toppled over on his face. But he flew up on a fence post and crowed. He'd et more corn than Sam. I wanted to break the news to boys on Raccoon Creek that my rooster had outet their champion eater. But I had to get on a mule and get a doctor.

"A man's a fool that will do a thing like this," Doc Hornbuckle said. "A big fine lookin' man like Sam Whiteapple ought to have more sense than to eat corn with the chickens. Swallowin' corn grains that have never been chewed. Get him home!"

I harnessed the mules and hitched them to the spring wagon. Doc helped me load Sam on the wagon. Doc strained his back liftin' on Sam. Finally we got him on the spring wagon, and I hauled him to Raccoon Creek. I left him with his people. His Pa was awful mad at me about it. But I didn't have nothin' to do with my rooster eatin' more corn than Sam. I told his Pa that too. He said that his crop was in the weeds and he needed Sam's help.

It was a funny thing the way people talked when Sam was so bad off the next two weeks. We'd go there and sit up all night. We'd talk about the corn Sam swallered. Some thought that Sam would have to swallow pieces of broken dishes, egg shells and white gravels from the creek just like a chicken did to work on the corn in Sam's craw. I told them Sam didn't have a craw and that Doc Hornbuckle would bring him out of it if anybody could, if they'd just listen to Doc's orders.

The last night I was over to the settinup, Doc Hornbuckle said, "Don't you ever try to outeat another chicken, Sam. You have ruint your stummick. You'll haf to go easy fer a year. You can't do much work. You'll just have to piddle about the place. I'm goin' to haf to put you on a cornflake diet. You'll haf to eat cornflakes and warm sweet milk mornin', noon and night."

Sam's eyes got awful big when Doc Hornbuckle said "cornflakes."

Through a College Window

by

WINIFRED BLAND

*W*inifred Bland, now a member of the J. B. Lippincott
company publishing staff, was a member of a class in
the short story at Middlebury College, Vermont, in 1933,
and when Sherwood Anderson's book of short stories, "Death
in the Woods," appeared, she read it and reviewed it. The
following is her review and she writes us, "the writing is
typically collegiate in most respects, or so it seems to me now.
My admiration for Sherwood Anderson's writing, however,
hasn't changed a particle." This review came to the attention
of Sherwood Anderson who saw in it the gratifying reaction
of his work among fresh young minds.

It is with great hesitation that I begin a review of this
book. I want to do it justice and I'm afraid it can't be done
in a cold literary analysis. The stories, themselves, are so
fresh and natural that they fairly leap from the pages when
you open the book. Indeed, when you read one of them, it
is as though you have given it a magic touch. The letters
integrate into a character, an experience, and walk around
Indian file after you—forever, I guess. But the point I
wanted to stress is that the stories are so simple that they are
tremendously complex, just as you can become terribly
fussed trying to answer a simple question like "Who am I?"

whereas a question on the causes of the Reformation might be answered at some length, tabulated too.

Sherwood Anderson's stories are queries into things that really count and his thought processes are clear and aboveboard. He wonders and you wonder along with him and then in the final twist, a sort of emotional push, you find yourself through the knothole, through the morass, through whatever he has gone through, and you feel decidedly wiser. It is just as though you had walked down a street fifteen hundred times and suddenly you happened to realize that every house in the block was wooden except one which was brick. And you puzzled and puzzled over what made that man build a brick house. So finally you went inside and asked the owner. And he would be so astonished that he would tell—some inane reason probably, some reason of inherited taste perhaps, some economical motive perhaps—but you'd feel better about it after you had done it.

However, the fact remains that there is enough substance to this book of stories to keep you busy forever and a day, cogitating, for the very simple reason that he has opened up a new world for you. From now on, if you could follow his leadership, you would really need no story books, for amusement anyway. You, yourself, would be creator; you would dare to look around you and notice things. Your life would be more intense, more full, and you would need fewer props, would be more self-sufficient.

There are just sixteen of these stories. Taken in chronological order, the first is about an old woman freezing to death. The second about a man returning to his home town after eighteen years. Number three is about a jealous husband worrying himself into a mild case of insanity. Four is a novelist's strange experience with a dream novel he never wrote. The fifth is a childhood enmity carried into an adult spite. The sixth is about an elderly, homely woman who walked through a patch of moonlight and suddenly seemed gloriously beautiful. The seventh is a sketch of would-be Bohemians. Eight is a philosophy professor's attempt to escape haunting memories by random travel. Nine, ten and eleven are glimpses of Kentucky mountain life which you sense are really genuine. The next one concerns a widower's emotions when he proposes a second time. Number thirteen is about an acquaintance struck up in New Orleans. Fourteen is a professor's futile attempt to achieve pure meditation, a failure he couldn't seem to regret. The fifteenth is a frank confession of a wife as to how she ensnared her husband. The last is about two kinds of death—death physically and death spiritually.

And there you have them all—each one a sort of vivisection of life. There are about four of them that struck me particularly hard. Already I have read them several times and each time I experienced the same tightened sensation in my throat. His best stories have a way of doing that to you. I remember one I read some time ago, before Sherwood Anderson was any more than a name. This one was called "I Am A Fool," and I wanted to cry and cry over it and all I could do was clench my fist and bite it.

I despise condensing stories into little cans to be opened at your leisure and poured into after-dinner coffee. I shan't do it. I'll just give the four names and try to tell why they made such a big impression.

The first was called "There She Is—She Is Taking Her Bath," and is chortlingly funny. The man telling the story has discovered that his wife is meeting a strange man. He tries to be subtle in his handling of the situation and only becames more and more involved. He has lived the sanest, plainest sort of life and the whole affair smacks so much of a triangle drama that he simply can't comprehend himself in the role of husband. When he tells the story, he has been living in this state of torment for two weeks and is fairly sputtering. He can't sleep, he can't work, and when he finally plucks up his courage to demand an explanation from his wife, she is taking a bath! Poor man, he is still trying to figure it all out and the story ends where it began. What bothers his almost as much as his wife's infidelity is the fact that it is interfering with his business. He can't concentrate on his real estate any more. Another significant fact is mentioned early in the story when he tells of hitting his head on the bathtub while shaving. You can't help wondering if perhaps

he isn't slightly unbalanced by it. All these colorings are
obtained by implication—not delicate hints, but rather casual
remarks to be taken at their face value or enlarged upon just
as you please.

The next one is called "A Meeting South" and stands out
in my mind as bewitchingly beautiful. The scene is in New
Orleans, where you have learned to expect romance, and
here you have a bit of it told realistically. How is this for
establishing an atmospheric footing?

"Evening was coming, the abrupt waning of the day and
the quick smoky soft-footed coming of night, characteristic
of the semi-tropic city, when he produced a bottle from his
hip pocket. It was so large that I was amazed. How had it
happened that the carrrying of so large a bottle had not made
him look deformed? 'Perhaps, like the kangaroo, his body has
developed some kind of a natural pouch for taking care of
supplies,' I thought. Really he walked as one might fancy a
kangaroo would walk when out for a quiet evening stroll.
I went along thinking of Darwin and the marvels of Prohibi-
tion. 'We are a wonderful people, we Americans,' I thought.
We were both in fine humor and had begun to like each
other immensely."

I didn't mean to go so far in quoting, but then I suddenly
realized what Sherwood Anderson's atmosphere is made up
of. Not a compound of dew and cobweb and sunbeam, but
rather a sort of homebrew of distilled humor, poetry, philosophy, and could you call it horse-sense? Yes, I think I was
wiser than I realized in picking that paragraph, for the in-
gredients are all there.

We have read stories and stories about New Orleans. Here
it is, brought up to date, and yet it could have happened
elsewhere; the experience is just colored by the enviroment.
There are references to the river. Once he says it was like a
vast moving sidewalk slipping noiselessly into the darkness;
and again he says looking at the Mississippi at nght is like
creeping into a dark bedroom to look at a sleeping child.

This story is beautiful and shows a mood of the author,
a softened mood not usually detected. He *is* changeable—
that is why he is a good storyteller.

The third story is called "Brother Death," and is very beautiful too. The little boy, Ted, has some sort of heart disease which may cause him to die at any moment. He has to face this constantly. Everyone knows it and nobody but his sister can realize how it would react on him. They all want to say "No" to everything that might strain him. Mary wisely and instinctively knows that this is worse than actual death—this life of fear—and finally succeeds in making them leave him alone. The contrast with the elder brother who gives in to his father to secure his material inheritance is grandly brought out. You catch a glimpse of something worse than death. You have a glimpse of something dazingly bright and pure as a white pebble will stare up from a brook. It takes no education to realize that life on the older brother's plane is too cheap. I cannot put it better than the author does in the last sentence.

"It was, she finally thought, because having to die his kind of death, he never had to make the surrender his brother had made—to be sure of possessions, success, his time to command—would never have to face the more subtle and terrible death that had come to his older brother."

I am wondering if perhaps we don't die a thousand deaths each day we live. I wonder how many times I have died already. I wonder how much life there is in me. I wonder how much life there is under some of the elaborate masks I see around me. I wonder what I would do if I knew I must die within a year. Would I go on a drunken debauch? Would I turn saint? I hope I'd just consent to go on and face things, not let it change me. But I am wandering. This story then might seem to show Sherwood Anderson's explorations into psychology and ethics. His range is truly great, is it not?

The fourth story and my very, very best favorite is called "In A Strange Town." This one, more than any, made me most miserably happy or happily miserable (as you want to put it). When you can create a complex emotion like that I think you have touched C major on the great scale of things.

In this story you see fused all the elements of Anderson's storytelling genius. There are passages like this—"Most of us live our lives like toads, sitting perfectly still, under a plantain leaf. We are waiting for a fly to come our way. When it comes out darts the tongue. We nab it.

"That is all. We eat it.

"But how many questions to be asked that are never asked. Whence came the fly? Where was he going?

"The fly might be going to meet his sweetheart. He was stopped, a spider ate him."

I call that magnificent writing. It is so human, it is terrible. It gives the insignificant significance; it gives the vain humility. It is Walt Whitman in prose.

I can't seem to become coherent in this essay. I can't even wax eloquent. It brings me up to a sort of a halt. I am suddenly looking into the eyes of a wise-young-old-man; an old-young-wise boy. Indeed, in all his writings Sherwood Anderson has a certain boyishness. I spoke before of the complex simplicity of his stories. They are just that. It is embarrassing. Little boys are often embarrassing. They stare at you coolly and frankly and make some pertinent remark that makes your hair stand on end. You don't know how to take them, they make you squirm. Sometimes you suspect them of wanting to make you squirm but you still can't deny it.

Sherwood Anderson's whole methods smack of this boyishness. The form of his stories is almost negligible in outline but it is compact and firm in impression. He reminds you of a boy on a ramble through the country. Perhaps he is on his way to school. He loiters along the path, dragging his books on a strap. Every twig and rock must be examined. Every beetle must be watched. Pockets already bulging are added to. With a hop-skip here and a breathless run there, you follow a zigzag course with him. Sherwood Anderson in his manhood has kept all the joyousness of a tramp like this but he has added an objective greater than the stuffy little schoolhouse. He has found a tree along the road and after a certain length of time he makes for the grassy bank under that tree. There he empties his pockets and picks up each grimy souvenir in order to examine it. Then he stretches out full-length and cogitates.

In his cogitation he gives his mind free reign. I'm not certain what is involved in the so-called "stream of consciousness" school of writers; but I should imagine he would belong with them. He doesn't believe in starting at the beginning on page one and going to the end on page so-and-so. I can hear his saying, "Where is the beginning and where is the end? There is no such thing. Everything is relative." And so he begins where he happens to begin—sometimes near the end, sometimes near the beginning and then he weaves back and forth. That's the way you think anyway. You never sit down and go through a living problem logically and exactly. It's only in mathematics and exact sciences that you can do that. And that's the way you live too. You don't start out on a carefully mapped out route and follow every signpost to a certain destination.

In connection with this trait of Anderson's, I can't help remembering what a man once said concerning memory. He said he had a good memory because he made a practice of never lying and that cut down the strain on his memory. Sherwood Anderson has nothing he has to remember to conceal, nothing he is afraid to tell—and the result is that he has clear, brilliant thought processes. Each thought leads to the next in a sort of black and white pattern, colored with reds and blues of emotion. Also he preserves that challenging old-young stare which embarrasses you. It isn't that he has lead a blameless life. It's just that he hasn't learned to be ashamed of his natural tendencies. I envy him.

I remember saying once I thought Sherwood Anderson's genius lay in the short story. At present I think that is perfectly true. But I see no reason why a more mature Sherwood Anderson should not take up the field of the novel and conquer that too. He has all the will power to stick to it. But even if he never went any farther, I think this latest book of his places him way up in the field of modern fiction. His position as a novelist might remain in doubt but as a short story writer he has achieved his place in the sun.

We're All Fools

(for Sherwood Anderson)

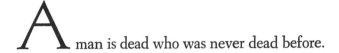 man is dead who was never dead before.

Let the legends awake now; for he is dead.
(It is a small thing to be born;
It is a poor end to do nothing but die.

So the fermented old lady at the bar surprised me
When she said would you like to meet a real live angel?
I said where is this angel? and she smiled a yellow smile,
Pointing to a lion which was asleep on the floor.
It was saddled all right but I didn't see any angel.
Are you ashamed of being afraid too?
We are too small to understand the ways of God.

Another time I saw a train run over a little girl.
She came out of the woods with her arms full of flowers.
Is that the kind of thing should happen?
People are afraid to say I am fed up.
People go by pairs into bed and cry together.)

But God invented racehorses

So as I was saying
As I was saying

I was saying that the world is all around us
And around the world is the water and
    through the water swims
A fish with a terrible eye
And people are fools to love racehorses

O men of little faith, salute one whose life was a flame;
May the gentle flowers of heaven fall on his upturned face.

KENNETH PATCHEN

A Man in Town

by

JAMES BOYD

I N my town, Southern Pines, there are twenty-six hundred people. The railroad runs down the main street but it is not as bad as you might think. On each side of it there are magnolias and shrubs put out by the Chamber of Commerce and then a fairly wide street and a sidewalk with sycamores and store fronts. Down the hill on the other side of the tracks the old houses are big and easy among big trees and further on down is the creek and on both sides of it the negro section. The little houses are pretty nice there, too, now. On this side of the tracks, up the hill, the new houses are spruce and suburban and U. S. No. 1 runs through. That is the town.

When Sherwood Anderson used to come here to stay he would walk down into the town, visit up and down the street, at the Broad Street Pharmacy, the depot, and Claude Hayes's Book Store and sit on the bench at the corner near the police station. Sometimes he would drive out into the country if I had to see somebody, or go over to the trotting horse barns at Pinehurst. Everywhere he went it was the same. Although nobody except Claude Hayes himself knew anything he had written, they knew he was a writer. But it made no difference, that is, no difference in the way they looked on him as a person. They had seen other writers around with me, Tom Wolfe and Scott Fitzgerald, and had liked them all right, but

as beings immediately recognizable as supernatural. Sherwood
they took for granted as a small-town American. How good
a thing to be that is, I leave to those able to balance Sinclair
Lewis' "Main Street" and William Allen White's "In Our
Town" and get a resultant formula. But whatever he may be,
the small-town man belongs to a fellowship which cuts
through sectional lines so that our people, Southerners with
a sprinkling of New Englanders and others, felt more at
home with Sherwood than they would have felt with a big-
town man from around here or from where they came from.
Often he said nothing, just listened. And when he was listening, his lips would move as though he were savoring what
was being said or commenting soundlessly. Then when he
said something it was simple and natural and inevitably right
for the small-town man to say. So everybody knew he was
one of themselves and, as is common, felt warmly toward him
and admired him for the ways, innumerable and often subtle
and microscopic, in which he was like themselves.

What made his position unique, though, was that they
admired him also for the ways in which he was not like
themselves. He was the small-town man, all right; they
understood that. But the small-town man has got some
natural limitations. He lives where, more than anywhere else
in the world, everybody knows his business, knows all about
him, at least all that can be found out. Since nobody can
stand too much of that, the small-town man is trained to keep
people from finding out too much. I won't say he's timid or
secretive any more than I would say so about a clam. It is just
that he has had to work out the only system on which he can
live. If he has, for intance, any inmost thoughts—as distinguished from ritual or jokes—about God, or women, he
keeps them to himself. The same is true, of course, of any
unusual ideas on any subjects. If you find a small-town man
expressing unusual ideas he is generally such a violently
unusual man that the rest of the people do not regard him as
a fellow townsman at all. At the worst they drive him out;
at the best, if he is lovable or bizarre or has some other merit,
they point to him with confused and secret pride as evidence
that the town can produce somebody who doesn't belong there

In Sherwood they found a person who was a small-town man, ordinarily one of the least free of creatures, and at the same time the freest man they had ever met. Like themselves he was kindly, easy-going, yet acute; he was full of inexhaustible interest in the most banal details of life and business, he was a master of the confused and meaningless clichés of small talk, and that was all good. But when the occasion seemed to merit it he would say simply but precisely what he thought on any subject. Say it with perfect freedom and integrity. That, they felt, was glorious. Here was a man in their own image who at the same time was honest with himself and moved and spoke in liberty. Who was, in short, what they might be. They were like negro slaves who meet a free negro. They felt that he had a meaning applicable to them.

That meaning was, I think, applicable to all the rest of us who knew him. His translucent and apparently spontaneous integrity toward his work, toward his mind and his spirit gave us an apocalyptic and perhaps deceptive view of how easy integrity might be. But by whatever pains arrived at, and however much we may have oversimplified the achievement of it, it did, I think, refresh and exalt us and healthfully shame us, too.

This integrity of his extended, so far as I could see, to every relationship. Toward other men he combined natural insight with affection and usually with serious respect. This respect in the face of an insight which included all their failings was, I think, the counterpart of his own humility, a humility which flowered from that same clear insight. Applied to himself and demonstrating, at least to his satisfaction, that in him, too, were the seeds of every failing to be found in others. In the presence of this wise and warm humility a man felt magically released. There was nothing that you could not say, no secret and sorry corner of your being that could not be disclosed. In any case it could not have been concealed from his penetrating eye. But concealment was as unnecessary as it was vain. All would be accepted as mere stigmata of man's fellowship and in the end he still would, if anything, believe you better, if not than you were, at least than you believed yourself.

Not that there was any bland and superficial composition
with evil in the lives of others, still less in his own. But there
was a complete acceptance of its existence, an almost matter-
of-fact recognition of its nature and a less certain but always
inspiring notion of what could be done to mitigate its effects
on the possessor, principally through the cleansing air of
honesty. Though how, in turn, others were to come by this
honesty, so apparently easy to him and so apparently effica-
cious, I was never able to learn.

Women, so far as I saw, loved him. Loved him, I suppose,
for his quiet warmth, for his apparent but quite illusory simplicity, for his genial indecencies, clean and sharp as salt, for
his eye and his sap. And he loved them with reserves, but
reserves not of a sort to alienate them. He looked on them
with affectionate compassion wholly devoid of patronage.
And indeed no patronage was possible in an attitude which
embraced not only unflagging interest but worship. No man
was ever more aware of women's presence in the world and
of its importance. No one had pondered more about the
whole baffling and glowing mystery or paid more homage to
its supernatural power for good and ill. But if they were for
him priestesses of a higher and more splendid mystery and
therefore to be reverenced, they were priestesses uninstructed
in the cult they served and tragically imprisoned in its ritual
so, therefore, to be taken with reserve and pitied.

Toward his own work his position would be a model for
any writer. He had been lauded, above all by other writers,
surely of all people those best qualified to measure his influence. And if, as so often happens in America, his work was
not sustained—none knew that better than he—his spirit
remained unaltered and continued to manifest itself in the
work of others if not in his own and to maintain him as a
figure of stature. Then suddenly he was reviled.

Book reviewing had become in its higher circles the vested
interest of Marxian dialecticians. Their thesis at the moment
was that the depression was to inaugurate the revolt of the
masses. At this unfortunate juncture, Sherwood, the small-
town man, driving his seedy car across the continent and talking to people, reported that the masses, if such could be said

to exist here, while confused and deeply perturbed, had no notion of revolting. For this inconvenient accuracy he was branded as a literary mountebank.

It is not necessary to pretend that neither praise nor blame affected a man so sensitive, so conscientious toward his calling. He felt both keenly, but he also felt that his responses were, so to speak, a private affair, having nothing to do with the real business on hand. That business, of course, was always and at whatever pains to write as well as he knew how. That was his sole responsibility and, having met it manfully, the rest, however it might affect his feelings, was not a proper subject for undue concern. It was not only a question of complete honesty in a man's work: a man besides should be firm and calm about how that work was received.

This honesty, good sense and simple strength that fortified his subtle complex mind equipped him singularly for all contacts. To his insight and sense of wonder, everything met was significant and unique; at the same time, to his sturdy innocence, nothing met was surprising. I have described his easy acceptance of the commonplace. And equally, again like the small-town American as seen, say, in foreign lands, he was at home and at ease when confronted by the bizarre.

In our house the unpredictable is likely. Once returning, I found him on the porch drinking Bourbon with the librarian of Princeton. There was some pretty learned talk going on about Elmer Adler and his print collection. The genial but grave proceedings were penetrated abruptly by the sound of girls singing. Looking through open door and windows to the other side of the house, we saw kilts and bonnets and young girls' figures whirling. Mr. Adler and his prints were dropped.

There is an excellent small woman's college near our home. Its name is Flora McDonald and it is filled with the daughters of the clans who came to North Carolina after Culloden. They dance their old Scots dances there and sometimes send away groups to give performances. My wife had intercepted such a group and asked them to come by and have refreshments. So, without warning, they were on our lawn, dancing for fun and singing a melody, as they had no other music.

Beneath their swinging kilts and sporans their bare knees twinkled, the silver buttons on their jackets twinkled as they locked their arms in a series of gestures, prescribed but gay. They paused for breath and danced again and as the dancing went on with pauses in between, Sherwood sitting among them twinkled, too. More than twinkled. Statically he made love to them. They felt it and loved him. The reverend gentleman in charge of the girls, sensing an altered atmospheric state, attempted by well-chosen remarks to establish what he conceived to be a higher plane. Then Sherwood and the girls secretly, together, were laughing at him. Warmly and knowingly. The girls had cookies and ginger ale then and all went home and I think that Sherwood never spoke to any of them. But I have thought of that moment as much as any I had with him and since his death I see him often as he was there, twinkling and shining, a delicate benign Silenus, a lion breathing cheer among the lambs. For in that moment he epitomized his qualities. He sat there, the small-town American whom we have seen in a thousand improbable conjunctions reducing, by his matter-of-factness and dry honesty, the unexpected to the level of the commonplace. Having made the reduction, it was Sherwood Anderson's genius to raise the moment, still within its comfortable frame, to something gay and lightly humorous and warm, to something touching and profound.

Go, Scholar-Gypsy!

by

BEN HECHT

BEN HECHT *wrote this piece for* PM *the day Sherwood Anderson sailed for South America. It is reprinted in* STORY *with the permission of the author who writes, "I am sorry I have neither the time nor the energy now to do one extra piece of writing. Anyway, whatever I did now that Sherwood is dead would be too much in the mood of an obit. I can't take these departures as lightly as I would wish."*

We sit in a saloon—Sherwood Anderson and I—at separate tables.

I haven't seen our Dostoevski of the corn belts for a long time. I note that his face has reddened and taken on a few more chins. His hair has silvered. But the black eyes still glitter like a card sharper's.

He is arrayed as of old, in something that looks more like a gunny sack than a suit. But, strike me blind, a white carnation festoons the left lapel. This gives him the air of a small-town barber on a spree—a jovial and archaic Wop who after the next drink will start warbling *Sole Mio.*

There is no Italian blood in Sherwood that anyone knows about—but for thirty years I have never seen a hurdy-gurdy man with a monkey or a village tonsorial expert that wasn't the spitting image of Sherwood.

147

Thirty years is a hell of a throw, but we go back that far together. I was a boy reporter in Chicago, but our Bard was already at grips with the Muse. He occupied an attic in Cass Street, drank red wine, loved candlelight, and was a sort of cross between a Yogi and a Lothario. I could never figure out whether he was going to found a religion or end up in jail for seduction. But he was too shrewd for either fate.

He used to read aloud his stories about Winesburg, Ohio, which seemed to me at the time very mystic and a little illiterate. I was busy learning grammar under the angry lash of a managing editor fresh from the highfalutin' tradition of the New York *Sun*. He was old Marty Hutchings, hallowed be his memory. And I felt I understood why nobody would buy Sherwood's tales about George Whoosthis. They were full of hanging participles.

This was in the time when Chicago was much like it is today—a city of literary darkness. Sherwood in his Cass Street attic, boring the pants off his disciples with third and fourth readings of his manuscripts, was the genius who was to turn that Smoke House town into the new Athens. Sherwood and a few others—among them a gentleman we called John Guts because he wrote poetry that not only did not rhyme but yapped violently and mystically at life. This was Carl Sandburg.

But chiefly it was Sherwood who was our genius. Sherwood was our Renaissance, our torch of letters, our Daniel Boone of Art. One day he was a secret known only to Margey Curry, Floyd Dell, Mike Carr, three swooning foreign girls, and me. And the next day he was Balzac, Tolstoy and Madame de Staël.

Trumpets pealed, prizes rained, honors covered him like another Scipio Africanus. "Windy MacPherson's Son," "Marching Men," "Winesburg, Ohio" (hanging participles and all) "Many Marriages," came banging out of his port side. The Midwest with a yell of "Anderson Forever" tucked a cutlass in its teeth and boarded the Victorian Era. We sort of sunk it.

I saw less of Sherwood then. He got tangled up in all kinds of Grand Tours. He wheeled around the country like a literary Durbar. Our Dark Horse had become Barnum and Bailey, but we felt no envy. We were all too busy becoming side shows.

Sitting in the saloon, I remember all this. I remember, too, that no one in my time has written as tenderly and deeply of small towns and small people. It was Sherwood who re-invented the American soul—dead since "David Harum." He found it in the milking shed, the hardware store, the village meeting hall, in the factory noon hour and on the front porch and touring in his Tin Lizzie.

I make a pilgrimage to Sherwood's table, as I will some day to his tomb, if I outlive him.

There is loud cackling from the Bard of Cass Street about my thinning hair and failing sight. This wattled old Telem-achus of letters, thrice a grandpa, would have it that I am his senior. And he laughs as of old (when age was never anything to be talked about) the same old water-whistle laugh. He is with a friend old enough to be father to both of us who takes up the ninnyish canard of my seniority. This other survival is George Jean Nathan. When the glee of these two Civil War veterans subsides, I ask Sherwood what he's up to.

"I'm leavin'," he says, and his black eyes glitter like Nick the Greek's with four aces in his hand. "I'm leavin' for South America. I'm goin' to Santiago, Chile, on a steamboat this Friday."

And Sherwood laughs, but this time not at me.

I inquire for how long.

"Oh, pretty long," says Sherwood, "maybe a year. Maybe two. Maybe forever."

I inquire what for.

"I don't know," says Sherwood. "You write why I'm goin'. If anybody ought to know about me, it's you. Write what you want," says Sherwood, and laughs again.

I ought to know and do. Sherwood is off to find something that vanished out of the world he knew and wrote about. It disappeared out of the West and East and even the South, where he went looking for it a few years ago. It was the American he knew—that moody, whimsical and inarticulate hero of the pre-radio, pre-movie hinterlands. Something scotched him. And Sherwood, his great biographer, is off for strange lands, where he can forget that his hero is dead.

Procession in the Rain

by

Manuel Komroff

About a hundred or more people walked in solemn procession through the streets of this little town. They were carrying a coffin. A slight drizzling rain filled the air.

I spoke to a stranger standing on the street beside me. "What is this?" I asked.

"A funeral," he replied, removing his hat.

"But I see no carriages or automobiles."

"For him they walk on foot."

"Out of respect?"

"Yes."

"They knew him so well?"

"Yes."

"They must have loved him."

"Yes, they love him and will always love him."

"And he knew them all?"

"Yes, he knew them well. He knew them even before they were born."

"Then he must have been very old."

"No. He was sixty-four."

"But some of these people seem even older. How could he have known them before they were born?"

"He did. He knew them all. He was like their father."

"How could a man be father to over a hundred people?"

"It may sound like a mystery to you, sir, but you are a stranger here. To us it is all very simple. These people you see marching bareheaded in the rain have gone all over the world and have visited many lands. They have returned for the funeral."

"Yes, that is indeed odd," I remarked.

By this time the procession had come to the place where we were standing. I removed my hat while the bier was passing.

The man beside me said, "He is not a stranger to you if you only knew. But if you want to know," he added, "I can tell you something that may indeed sound to you very strange. He who died is not in that coffin."

"What!" I exclaimed. "What then is in the coffin?"

"Nothing!"

"Then why do they carry it?"

"Because they are his children and they must bury him."

"This is more than I can stand! Some of the children are older than he and they are going to bury him, yet you say he is not in the coffin! All this is impossible!"

"It is all simple, if you only understood, sir."

"The man they are burying is the author of their being. He is their creator. They were born from his heart and brain. They are his creatures and once born they will never die. And now at this very moment they are putting his soul to rest."

"What is his name?"

"Sherwood Anderson."

"And what is the name of this town? I cannot find it on my road map."

"This town is as famous as any in this part of America. You are now in Winesburg, Ohio."

"What is this town famous for?"

"Here was born a new spirit in American literature. Here at the blacksmith shop the chains were broken. Here a liberation took place. It seemed so simple and so easy, and many were later to follow in the trail that he blazed. But it took a man of genius and one who loved his fellow creatures to do

it. It took understanding and a heart overflowing with sympathy for the lonely and the disinherited."

"And he was the one to do all this?"

"Yes; he was the one. His name is Sherwood Anderson."

Auction Day In Missouri

By

Ferner Nuhn

W<small>E HAD</small> stopped for lunch in a northern Missouri town a few weeks after Anderson's death. It happened to be on a livestock auction day. The town was full of farmers and their families in for trading. There was a continuous drift from the town square where the stores were, down a side street to the auction barn. The air was festive. We were glad we had stopped.

There is a special quality to the people of this middle border, I mean the border between north and south along the hill and river country from western Virginia to Missouri and Arkansas. Something of the early forest life still clings to them, a liking for independence—also the pleasure in gregariousness visible on occasions such as this one. They are too poor to make up anything but a one-class society. On this day all wore their ordinary farm clothes. The faces were butternut-brown, seamy, with kindly rather more than harsh lines. The voices, like the eyes, were soft. It was plain they enjoyed talking and their speech was full of concrete details from daily life. One heard a vein of natural poetry in it too.

As we walked down to the stock barn and stood for a while with the crowd listening to the auctioneer, I kept thinking of

Anderson. His essence was somehow in the air; I almost could see him here, a "man going around" as he liked to say of himself, listening, observing, talking. These were his people: from this strain we had got Lincoln, and Mark Twain, the hill songs and stories, hundreds of quirks of thought and speech—and Sherwood Anderson. This plainly was his kind of day and occasion; I felt him enjoying the atmosphere of common festivity full of real human affairs but touched with celebration.

And all about I felt an actual liking for the fellow human being. It is at the core of this strain: it was in Lincoln, in Whitman; it was in Anderson and kept growing in his work. So for the middle-border American, democracy is an organic thing. Indeed is there any other quality on which it possibly can rest?

Spring, 1941

by

MARSDEN HARTLEY

Dear Sherwood:

They have asked me to write something about you. But I said to myself—if I attempt to write about him as an author, I'll have to admit to an appalling case of craft-ignorance. It would be the same in reference to several of my friends who are authors—Eugene O'Neill, Waldo Frank and others. Let their brothers who compose plays and novels criticize them.

So I decided to write to you, having something to say about you and to you. I've been reading "Winesburg, Ohio"— I don't know how I lived so long without the sense of the book's lyrical perfection. And I've been out for a walk in the country.

It was a rainy day, a lovely rainy day. Everything smelled fresh and sweet under the trees in the softly, gently falling showers: fresh and sweet, exciting and warm. With the spirit and the senses out and filled with warm, pulsing earth, I found myself saying "I know a man related to all these things. His name is Anderson."

If ever anyone was made of earth and for the earth, Sherwood, it is yourself. I say "is" for the reason that I have come to think factual finalities insignificant in the fuller sense. You certainly were one of those who seem always to have been there. I never considered it any use trying to fix dates in the matter of friendship—and even if I could fix the date of our meetings, which I cannot, I would say "What of it? There never was a time when he wasn't there."

It has been a wonderful spring and I walked out into the country. There were the layers of the pinkish and white dog-wood against the branches of the spruce, and close to the ground fully furled leaves of skunk-cabbages, hanging bells of dog-tooth violets, scatterings of spring beauties in the grass. There were blue violets and the small white variety—all the galaxy which assists in the sacred process of spring. In this hour of tribulation of the human spirit, in the face of the unspeakably harrowing, it was good to look on these innocent harbingers of the good life. They know nothing but the cor-rect behavior of decent things. Hasn't the way of art always lain over their perfect petals? Great God, Sherwood, the pity and more than pity, the shame of this hour!

Well, I wished then you hadn't gone the way you did, the way that fate insisted you go. After all, the tricks of a tooth-pick are scarcely to be recognized as dignified. I was reminded of a singer friend of mine, a big beautiful woman with a rich voice and the small feet so many large people have. She overtook my ear one day with a blast of rage because she had tripped on the edge of a rug or a strip of lamp wire. The words she used were quoted from Emerson, or was it the Upanishads? They were: "If there's anything I cannot stand it is the cussedness of inanimate objects." That toothpick was certainly one of those objects with a terrible fatality of purpose.

Still as you already have gathered, Sherwood, I am getting kick upon kick from the plausible notion of immortality. Only yesterday I received a letter from Mme. Lachaise, and speaking of the spring she had added "I cannot think La-chaise will not come again," and I promptly replied "He is there already, has not gone away." This has nothing what-ever to do with attempts at cultish belief. Rather it's the feeling left in us by people who love us and whom we love. You, I always felt, were one of those warm beings who live

all over themselves when they say something or even when
they say nothing. (How tiresome head-talk can be, when
nothing happens beneath the chin, we all know.) . . . I could
hear the deep rich rumble of your voice sounding like the
grind of big wooden wheels over a sandy road before a
shower, or like the dark and song-like vocalisms of a wide
quick river.

There were the wild flowers; I found Winesburg too in
them. They also were sincere—or should I have compared
the book's naturalness to Ty Cobb's clearing the bases with
a home run? You were a truth-telling story-teller—the truth
being always a story—there never being a place where people come together where there isn't a story to be set down.
That you were, I dare assert—and it is another reason why
I think it foolish to say "good-bye" to you and consider the
terms "so long" and "I'll be seeing you" appropriate to the
situation.

POSTSCRIPT

they say you went
over some awkward tropic
hill—
well, the sense of sacrament
is the same
no matter where its signature
fell—

I never did take too much
stock, in death
or the loss of high-priced
breath
one thing being equal to another-
why bother?
But feeling you opposite
the portal of my explicit self,
I feel the lushness of your

bright hardihood
the glory of the driven blood
which is the aspect of inheritance
of this given space.

Sherwood, when we do meet—
you know—hook up in that
highly oriented place
we hear so much of—and no
one seems to have the clue
to state its fabulous case,
well—shan't we go on
and discuss
the taut measure of this universe,
find roundness for our earth-bound
angular discourse
and most of all, real chance
to quietly dispose of earth
Dullness?

No doubt. So I'll say
We'll be seeing you
Another day.
—The Sky is lovely now.

The Triumph of The Egg

by

SHERWOOD ANDERSON

My father was, I am sure, intended by nature to be a cheerful, kindly man. Until he was thirty-four years old he worked as a farm hand for a man named Thomas Butterworth whose place lay near the town of Bidwell, Ohio. He had then a horse of his own and on Saturday evenings drove into town to spend a few hours in social intercourse with other farm hands. In town he drank several glasses of beer and stood about in Ben Head's saloon—crowded on Saturday evenings with visiting farm hands. Songs were sung and glasses thumped on the bar. At ten o'clock father drove home along a lonely country road, made his horse comfortable for the night and himself went to bed, quite happy in his position in life. He had at that time no notion of trying to rise in the world.

It was in the spring of his thirty-fifth year that father married my mother, then a country schoolteacher, and in the following spring I came wriggling and crying into the world. Something happened to the two people. They became ambitious. The American passion for getting up in the world took possession of them.

It may have been that mother was responsible. Being a schoolteacher she had no doubt read books and magazines. She had, I presume, read of how Garfield, Lincoln, and other

161

Americans rose from poverty to fame and greatness and as I lay beside her—in the days of her lying-in—she may have dreamed that I would some day rule men and cities. At any rate she induced father to give up his place as a farm hand, sell his horse and embark on an independent enterprise of his own. She was a tall silent woman with a long nose and troubled gray eyes. For herself she wanted nothing. For father and myself she was incurably ambitious.

The first venture into which the two people went turned out badly. They rented ten acres of poor stony land on Griggs's Road, eight miles from Bidwell, and launched into chicken raising. I grew into boyhood on the place and got my first impressions of life there. From the beginning they were impressions of disaster and if, in my turn, I am a gloomy man inclined to see the darker side of life, I attribute it to the fact that what should have been for me the happy joyous days of childhood were spent on a chicken farm.

One unversed in such matters can have no notion of the many and tragic things that can happen to a chicken. It is born out of an egg, lives for a few weeks as a tiny fluffy thing such as you will see pictured on Easter cards, then becomes hideously naked, eats quantities of corn and meal bought by the sweat of your father's brow, gets diseases called pip, cholera, and other names, stands looking with stupid eyes at the sun, becomes sick and dies. A few hens and now and then a rooster, intended to serve God's mysterious ends, struggle through to maturity. The hens lay eggs out of which come other chickens and the dreadful cycle is thus made complete. It is all unbelievably complex. Most philosophers must have been raised on chicken farms. One hopes for so much from a chicken and is so dreadfully disillusioned. Small chickens, just setting out on the journey of life, look so bright and alert and they are in fact so dreadfully stupid. They are so much like people they mix one up in one's judgments of life. If disease does not kill them they wait until your expectations are thoroughly aroused and then walk under the wheels of a wagon—to go squashed and dead back to their maker. Vermin infest their youth, and fortunes must be spent for curative powders. In later life I have seen how a literature has been built up on the subject of fortunes to be made out of the raising of chickens. It is intended to be read by the gods who have just eaten of the tree of the knowledge of good and evil. It is a hopeful literature and declares that much may be done by simple ambitious people who own a few hens. Do not be led astray by it. It was not written for you. Go hunt for gold on the frozen hills of Alaska, put your faith in the honesty of a politician, believe if you will that the world is daily growing better and that good will triumph over evil, but do not read and believe the literature that is written concerning the hen. It was not written for you.

I, however, digress. My tale does not primarily concern itself with the hen. If correctly told it will center on the egg. For ten years my father and mother struggled to make our chicken farm pay and then they gave up that struggle and began another. They moved into the town of Bidwell, Ohio and embarked in the restaurant business. After ten years of worry with incubators that did not hatch, and with tiny— and in their own way lovely—balls of fluff that passed on into semi-naked pullethood and from that into dead henhood, we threw all aside and packing our belongings on a wagon drove down Griggs's Road toward Bidwell, a tiny caravan of hope looking for a new place from which to start on our upward journey through life.

We must have been a sad looking lot, not, I fancy, unlike refugees fleeing from a battlefield. Mother and I walked in the road. The wagon that contained our goods had been borrowed for the day from Mr. Albert Griggs, a neighbor. Out of its sides stuck the legs of cheap chairs and at the back of the pile of beds, tables, and boxes filled with kitchen utensils was a crate of live chickens, and on top of that the baby carriage in which I had been wheeled about in my infancy. Why we stuck to the baby carriage I don't know. It was unlikely other children would be born and the wheels were broken. People who have few possessions cling tightly to those they have. That is one of the facts that make life so discouraging.

Father rode on top of the wagon. He was then a bald-headed man of forty-five, a little fat and from long association with mother and the chickens he had become habitually silent and discouraged. All during our ten years on the chicken farm he had worked as a laborer on neighboring farms and most of the money he had earned had been spent for remedies to cure chicken diseases, on Wilmer's White Wonder Cholera Cure or Professor Bidlow's Egg Producer or some other preparations that mother found advertised in the poultry papers. There were two little patches of hair on father's head just above his ears. I remember that as a child I used to sit looking at him when he had gone to sleep in a chair before the stove on Sunday afternoons in the winter. I had at that time already begun to read books and have notions of my own and the bald path that led over the top of his head was, I fancied, something like a broad road, such a road as Caesar might have made on which to lead his legions out of Rome and into the wonders of an unknown world. The tufts of hair that grew above father's ears were, I thought, like forests. I fell into a half-sleeping, half-waking state and dreamed I was a tiny thing going along the road into a far, beautiful place where there were no chicken farms and where life was a happy eggless affair.

One might write a book concerning our flight from the chicken farm into town. Mother and I walked the entire eight miles—she to be sure that nothing fell from the wagon and I to see the wonders of the world. On the seat of the wagon beside father was his greatest treasure. I will tell you of that.

On a chicken farm where hundreds and even thousands of chickens come out of eggs surprising things sometimes happen. Grotesques are born out of eggs as out of people. The accident does not often occur—perhaps once in a thousand births. A chicken is, you see, born that has four legs, two pairs of wings, two heads or what not. The things do not live. They go quickly back to the hand of their maker that has for a moment trembled. The fact that the poor little things could not live was one of the tragedies of life to father. He had some sort of notion that if he could but bring into henhood or roosterhood a five-legged hen or a two-headed rooster his fortune would be made. He dreamed of taking the wonder about to county fairs and of growing rich by exhibiting it to other farm hands.

At any rate he saved all the little monstrous things that had been born on our chicken farm. They were preserved in alcohol and put each in its own glass bottle. These he had carefully put into a box and on our journey into town it was carried on the wagon seat beside him. He drove the horses with one hand and with the other clung to the box. When we got to our destination the box was taken down at once and the bottles removed. All during our days as keepers of a restaurant in the town of Bidwell, Ohio, the grotesques in their little glass bottles sat on a shelf back of the counter. Mother sometimes protested but father was a rock on the subject of his treasure. The grotesques were, he declared, valuable. People, he said, liked to look at strange and wonderful things.

Did I say that we embarked in the restaurant business in the town of Bidwell, Ohio? I exaggerated a little. The town itself lay at the foot of a low hill and on the shore of a small river. The railroad did not run through the town and the station was a mile away to the north at a place called Pickleville. There had been a cider mill and pickle factory at the station, but before the time of our coming they had both gone out of business. In the morning and in the evening busses came down to the station along a road called Turner's Pike from the hotel on the main street of Bidwell. Our going to the out of the way place to embark in the restaurant business was mother's idea. She talked of it for a year and then one day went off and rented an empty store building opposite the railroad station. It was her idea that the restaurant would be profitable. Traveling men, she said, would be always waiting around to take trains out of town and town people would come to the station to await incoming trains. They would come to the restaurant to buy pieces of pie and drink coffee. Now that I am older I know that she had another motive in going. She was ambitious for me. She wanted me to rise in the world, to get into a town school and become a man of the towns.

At Pickleville father and mother worked hard as they always had done. At first there was the necessity of putting our

place into shape to be a restaurant. That took a month. Father
built a shelf on which he put tins of vegetables. He painted
a sign on which he put his name in large red letters. Below
his name was the sharp command—"EAT HERE"—that was
so seldom obeyed. A show case was bought and filled with
cigars and tobacco. Mother scrubbed the floor and the walls
of the room. I went to school in the town and was glad to be
away from the farm and from the presence of the discouraged,
sad-looking chickens. Still I was not very joyous. In the evening I walked home from school along Turner's Pike and
remembered the children I had seen playing in the town
school yard. A troop of little girls had gone hopping about
and singing. I tried that. Down along the frozen road I went
hopping solemnly on one leg. "Hippity Hop To The Barber
Shop," I sang shrilly. Then I stopped and looked doubtfully
about. I was afraid of being seen in my gay mood. It must
have seemed to me that I was doing a thing that should not
be done by one who, like myself, had been raised on a
chicken farm where death was a daily visitor.

Mother decided that our restaurant should remain open at
night. At ten in the evening a passenger train went north
past our door followed by a local freight. The freight crew
had switching to do in Pickleville and when the work was
done they came to our restaurant for hot coffee and food.
Sometimes one of them ordered a fried egg. In the morning
at four they returned northbound and again visited us. A little
trade began to grow up. Mother slept at night and during the
day tended the restaurant and fed our boarders while father
slept. He slept in the same bed mother had occupied during
the night and I went off to the town of Bidwell and to school.
During the long nights, while mother and I slept, father
cooked meats that were to go into sandwiches for the lunch
baskets of our boarders. Then an idea in regard to getting up
in the world came into his head. The American spirit took
hold of him. He also became ambitious.

In the long nights when there was little to do father had
time to think. That was his undoing. He decided that he had
in the past been an unsuccessful man because he had not
been cheerful enough and that in the future he would adopt

a cheerful outlook on life. In the early morning he came upstairs and got into bed with mother. She woke and the two talked. From my bed in the corner I listened.

It was father's idea that both he and mother should try to entertain the people who came to eat at our restaurant. I cannot now remember his words, but he gave the impression of one about to become in some obscure way a kind of public entertainer. When people, particularly young people from the town of Bidwell, came into our place, as on very rare occasions they did, bright entertaining conversation was to be made. From father's words I gathered that something of the jolly innkeeper effect was to be sought. Mother must have been doubtful from the first, but she said nothing discouraging. It was father's notion that a passion for the company of himself and mother would spring up in the breasts of the younger people of the town of Bidwell. In the evening bright happy groups would come singing down Turner's Pike. They would troop shouting with joy and laughter into our place. There would be song and festivity. I do not mean to give the impression that father spoke so elaborately of the matter. He was as I have said an uncommunicative man. "They want some place to go. I tell you they want some place to go," he said over and over. That was as far as he got. My own imagination has filled in the blanks.

For two or three weeks this notion of father's invaded our house. We did not talk much, but in our daily lives tried earnestly to make smiles take the place of glum looks. Mother smiled at the boarders and I, catching the infection, smiled at our cat. Father became a little feverish in his anxiety to please. There was no doubt, lurking somewhere in him, a touch of the spirit of the showman. He did not waste much of his ammunition on the railroad men he served at night but seemed to be waiting for a young man or woman from Bidwell to come in to show what he could do. On the counter in the restaurant there was a wire basket kept always filled with eggs, and it must have been before his eyes when the idea of being entertaining was born in his brain. There was something prenatal about the way eggs kept themselves connected with the development of his idea. At any rate an egg

ruined his new impulse in life. Late one night I was awak-
ened by a roar of anger coming from father's throat. Both
mother and I sat upright in our beds. With trembling hands
she lighted a lamp that stood on a table by her head. Downstairs the front door of our restaurant went shut with a bang
and in a few minutes father tramped up the stairs. He held
an egg in his hand and his hand trembled as though he were
having a chill. There was a half insane light in his eyes. As
he stood glaring at us I was sure he intended throwing the
egg at either mother or me. Then he laid it gently on the
table beside the lamp and dropped on his knees beside
mother's bed. He began to cry like a boy and I, carried away
by his grief, cried with him. The two of us filled the little
upstairs room with our wailing voices. It is ridiculous, but of
the picture we made I can remember only the fact that
mother's hand continually stroked the bald path that ran
across the top of his head. I have forgotten what mother said
to him and how she induced him to tell her of what had
happened downstairs. His explanation also has gone out of
my mind. I remember only my own grief and fright and the
shiny path over father's head glowing in the lamplight as he
knelt by the bed.

As to what happened downstairs. For some unexplainable
reason I know the story as well as though I had been a
witness to my father's discomfiture. One in time gets to know
many unexplainable things. On that evening young Joe
Kane, son of a merchant of Bidwell, came to Pickleville to
meet his father, who was expected on the ten o'clock evening
train from the South. The train was three hours late and Joe
came into our place to loaf about and to wait for its arrival.
The local freight train came in and the freight crew were fed.
Joe was left alone in the restaurant with father.

From the moment he came into our place the Bidwell
young man must have been puzzled by my father's actions.
It was his notion that father was angry at him for hanging
around. He noticed that the restaurant keeper was apparently
disturbed by his presence and he thought of going out.
However, it began to rain and he did not fancy the long
walk to town and back. He bought a five-cent cigar and

ordered a cup of coffee. He had a newspaper in his pocket and took it out and began to read. "I'm waiting for the evening train. It's late," he said apologetically.

For a long time father, whom Joe Kane had never seen before, remained silently gazing at his visitor. He was no doubt suffering from an attack of stage fright. As so often happens in life he had thought so much and so often of the situation that now confronted him that he was somewhat nervous in its presence.

For one thing, he did not know what to do with his hands. He thrust one of them nervously over the counter and shook hands with Joe Kane. "How-de-do," he said. Joe Kane put his newspaper down and stared at him. Father's eye lighted on the basket of eggs that sat on the counter and he began to talk. "Well," he began hesitatingly, "well, you have heard of Christopher Columbus, eh?" He seemed to be angry. "That Christopher Columbus was a cheat," he declared emphatically. "He talked of making an egg stand on its end. He talked, he did, and then he went and broke the end of the egg."

My father seemed to his visitor to be beside himself at the duplicity of Christopher Columbus. He muttered and swore. He declared it was wrong to teach children that Christopher Columbus was a great man when, after all, he cheated at the critical moment. He had declared he would make an egg stand on end and then when his bluff had been called he had done a trick. Still grumbling at Columbus, father took an egg from the basket on the counter and began to walk up and down. He rolled the egg between the palms of his hands. He smiled genially. He began to mumble words regarding the effect to be produced on an egg by the electricity that comes out of the human body. He declared that without breaking its shell and by virtue of rolling it back and forth in his hands he could stand the egg on its end. He explained that the warmth of his hands and the gentle rolling movement he gave the egg created a new center of gravity, and Joe Kane was mildly interested. "I have handled thousands of eggs," father said. "No one knows more about eggs than I do."

He stood the egg on the counter and it fell on its side. He

tried the trick again and again, each time rolling the egg
between the palms of his hands and saying the words regarding the wonders of electricity and the laws of gravity. When
after a half hour's effort he did succeed in making the egg
stand for a moment he looked up to find that his visitor was
no longer watching. By the time he had succeeded in calling
Joe Kane's attention to the success of his effort the egg had
again rolled over and lay on its side.

Afire with the showman's passion and at the same time a
good deal disconcerted by the failure of his first effort, father
now took the bottle containing the poultry monstrosities
down from their place on the shelf and began to show them
to his visitor. "How would you like to have seven legs and
two heads like this fellow?" he asked, exhibiting the most
remarkable of his treasures. A cheerful smile played over his
face. He reached over the counter and tried to slap Joe Kane
on the shoulder as he had seen men do in Ben Head's saloon
when he was a young farm hand and drove to town on Saturday evenings. His visitor was made a little ill by the sight of
the body of the terribly deformed bird floating in the alcohol
in the bottle and got up to go. Coming from behind the
counter father took hold of the young man's arm and led him
back to his seat. He grew a little angry and for a moment had
to turn his face away and force himself to smile. Then he put
the bottles back on the shelf. In an outburst of generosity
he fairly compelled Joe Kane to have a fresh cup of coffee and
another cigar at his expense. Then he took a pan and filling it
with vinegar, taken from a jug that sat beneath the counter,
he declared himself about to do a new trick. "I will heat this
egg in this pan of vinegar," he said. "Then I will put it
through the neck of a bottle without breaking the shell.
When the egg is inside the bottle it will resume its normal
shape and the shell will become hard again. Then I will give
the bottle with the egg in it to you. You can take it about
with you wherever you go. People will want to know how
you got the egg in the bottle. Don't tell them. Keep them
guessing. That is the way to have fun with this trick."

Father grinned and winked at his visitor. Joe Kane decided
that the man who confronted him was mildly insane but

harmless. He drank the cup of coffee that had been given him and began to read his paper again. When the egg had been heated in vinegar father carried it on a spoon to the counter and going into a back room got an empty bottle. He was angry because his visitor did not watch him as he began to do his trick, but nevertheless went cheerfully to work. For a long time he struggled, trying to get the egg to go through the neck of the bottle. He put the pan of vinegar back on the stove, intending to reheat the egg, then picked it up and burned his fingers. After a second bath in the hot vinegar the shell of the egg had been softened a little but not enough for his purpose. He worked and worked and a spirit of desperate determination took possession of him. When he thought that at last the trick was about to be consummated the delayed train came in at the station and Joe Kane started to go nonchalantly out at the door. Father made a last desperate effort to conquer the egg and make it do the thing that would establish his reputation as one who knew how to entertain guests who came into his restaurant. He worried the egg. He attempted to be somewhat rough with it. He swore and the sweat stood out on his forehead. The egg broke under his hand. When the contents spurted over his clothes, Joe Kane, who had stopped at the door, turned and laughed.

A roar of anger rose from my father's throat. He danced and shouted a string of inarticulate words. Grabbing another egg from the basket on the counter, he threw it, just missing the head of the young man as he dodged through the door and escaped.

Father came upstairs to mother and me with an egg in his hand. I do not know what he intended to do. I imagine he had some idea of destroying it, of destroying all eggs, and that he intended to let mother and me see him begin. When, however, he got into the presence of mother something happened to him. He laid the egg gently on the table and dropped on his knees by the bed as I have already explained. He later decided to close the restaurant for the night and to come upstairs and get into bed. When he did so he blew out the light and after much muttered conversation both he and mother went to sleep. I suppose I went to sleep also, but my sleep was troubled. I awoke at dawn and for a long time looked at the egg that lay on the table. I wondered why eggs had to be and why from the egg came the hen who again laid the egg. The question got into my blood. It has stayed there, I imagine, because I am the son of my father. At any rate, the problem remains unsolved in my mind. And that, I conclude, is but another evidence of the complete and final triumph of the egg—at least as far as my family is concerned.

The Modern Writer

by

SHERWOOD ANDERSON

The Modern Writer *

by

Sherwood Anderson

After all it is not very strange that we in America have been a long time coming to the beginning of something like a national literature. Nations are not made in a short time and we Americans have been trying to make rather a large nation. In a compact small country in which for hundreds of years the same people have lived, slowly building up traditions, telling old tales, singing old songs, the story teller or the poet has something in which he can rest. People grown old, as a people, on the same land, through which old rivers flow, looking out for generations upon the same great plains and up into the same mountains, come to know each other in an intimate way unknown to us here. The son following in the footsteps of a father dreams old dreams. The land itself whispers to him. Stories are in the very air about the writer. They spring up out of the soil on which for many hundreds of years people of one blood have been born, have lived, suffered, had moments of happiness and have died.

In America the writer is faced with a situation that is

---

* The reader should bear in mind that this essay was originally published in 1925 when such reference as the time it took to fly from New York to California may appear strange in light of present day flight schedules. The other remarks relating to that period in no way detract from the cogency of the theme as applied to the writer's problems today.—Ed.

unique. Our country is vast. In it are to be found so many
different conditions of life, so many different social traditions
that the writer who attempts to express in his work something
national is in an almost impossible position. At best, as yet,
he can only snatch at fragments. California is not Maine.
North Dakota is not Louisiana. Ohio is not North Carolina.
We are as yet strangers to each other. We are all of us just
a little afraid of each other. Time only can weld us together,
make us one people, make us understand each other. And in
understanding alone is the real love of comrades, that is the
beginning of a real love of our country.

Now I am an American writer and I have been by critics
in general classed among that rather vague group known as
the Moderns. I have set myself here to speak to you on the
subject of modern American writing. The whole business of
expressing definite opinions is new to me. I am in my nature
a teller of tales, not a preacher, and I have been told that in
trying to address any considerable number of people on a
large subject it is a mistake to try to cover too much ground,
that the writer should confine himself to the making of a few
points, but how I am to do that on such a subject as Modern-
ism I do not know. As a matter of fact I have, within the last
year, written a book on the subject, a book called *A Story
Teller's Story* and in it there are I believe something like
a hundred and thirty thousand words. Now that the book,
half a tale, half an attempt to put down certain notions
of my own, is written, I look forward eagerly to the getting
of my hands on the proofs. There are so many things I shall
not succeed in getting said, even in a large book.

As everyone knows, there is in the world at this time what
is broadly termed a Modern movement. It has expressed itself
in a great many ways. In a short time within the last fifteen or
twenty years, it has practically revolutionized painting all over
the world. It has crept into the writing of prose, into the
making of song, into sculpture, into architecture. Although
you may not realize it the fact is that the neckties worn by
many men in our city streets and the dresses worn by the
women have been influenced by the movement. The street
scene of the American city is becoming more colorful, designs

are bolder. The modern movement is beginning to express itself in buildings. In our residences we are less inclined to copy the impulses of old lands. Architecture, long one of the most dead and dreary of the arts as practiced in America, is becoming alive. It will become every year, I believe, more alive.

But it would be impossible for me, in a short article to speak in any general way on so broad a subject. It will be enough if I can give you some notions of what the present day American writer is faced with, what conditions he has to meet, what difficulties are to be overcome, what in my opinion is making American writing so bad and what in present day conditions tends to make it better.

As no man can speak of the writing of a country without saying something of the history of the intellectual life of the country, I shall have to begin by speaking of that.

It is, I think, pretty well understood among us that the intellectual life of America had its home nest in New England. Our culture is as yet a puritanical New England culture. The New England states, all cold, hard and stony, produced a rather cold and stony culture, but the New Englander, like so many repressed and defeated peoples, was intellectually energetic. He spread his notion of life out over the country. Living as he did in a land where the ground was cold and comparatively unproductive underfoot and the skies cold and forbidding overhead, he spent a great deal of his time cultivating God. His art impulse was non-sensual, intellectual. Life to the New Englander was not to be lived here and now. Life was to be spent in preparation for a life after death. Love of his fellow man did not enter into the New Englander's scheme, and the arts were made the servants of morality. There was so much of life of which the New Englander was forbidden to speak, toward which he did not dare be too sympathetic that as a result and while New England ruled, gentility and respectability became the passion of our writers. In literature sins might be committed in France or in some vague place far away like the South Seas, but among the heroes and heroines of the writer's fancy there must be no sin. As that was a quite impossible supposition, in as much as the writer must after all deal with human beings, the writers found a way out. The "good" and the "bad" man notion was played up to the limit. Women in books became all virgins or adventuresses. The good man had a hard struggle before him but he always ended by getting rich and marrying the virgin, after almost falling into the clutches of the adventuress. The puritanic mind was satisfied. It was made happy. The man reader of the books could always in the end follow with satisfaction the fancy of the writer and end by becoming a millionaire and the woman reader could in fancy get married, not as so often happens in real life by using methods that would shock the puritan beyond recovery, but simply by virtue of inherent goodness and virginity. It was a kind of patent formula that always worked in books. And in books and in the movies it still works pretty well. If any of you want to become writers and want to succeed it is still the best of all formulas to follow.

It all fitted in so neatly, you see.

For while in our schools and colleges and in our literature the puritan, the New Englander ruled, people were pouring into America from all over western Europe. The cold blood of the men of the North was being mixed constantly with the warmer blood of the South. Italians came. The Greeks and the southern Slavs came in hundreds of thousands. The eager highly temperamental Jews and the imaginative Celts poured in. On the West coast they got the Spaniard and the Mexican, and no man ever, I believe, accused the Spaniard or the Mexican of being puritanic.

The intellectual life of the country was being formed and controlled by English Protestants while the physical American was being built up of a mixture of all of the bloods of the western world and the process is still, I believe, going on. In our political thought the Adamses of New England, with their desire to establish an intellectual aristocracy, are still, I believe, more powerful than Lincoln the artist democrat, and, although by the world in general Whitman is recognized as our one great American poet, I have heard of no general movement to introduce him into our public schools to take the place of the decidedly second rate and imitative New Englander, Longfellow.

I am sure that almost everyone nowadays knows that there is at this moment something happening in the spiritual life of the American people. In the first place, there has been for a long time now, and particularly among our younger men and women, a rather intense boredom with the more obvious impulses of our American life. There is a new restlessness that is more and more expressing itself in individual revoluton against the social laws and customs of another age. Old gods are dead and we have all gone hunting new gods. Men and women are seeking expression for their lives in new and bolder ways and everywhere among writers the Modern is but the man who is trying to give expression to the newer impulses of our lives in books, in song, in painting and in all the others of the seven arts.

You must understand of course that as a nation we have put something across. Coming to America as we did, in reality scattered herds of peoples from dozens of European countries, often not speaking the same language, not having back of us the same traditions, spreading ourselves out rapidly over a vast country, cutting down forests, building railroads and bridges over rivers, mountains and deserts, learning to know each other a little in the process, building cities and towns, making the mines produce, making the land produce, we had for a long time need of all our energies for purely physical purposes. A poet or a painter in California in '49 or in the middle west in Abraham Lincoln's day would have been a nuisance and a pest.

A man I know was during the war arrested and sent to jail for being opposed to war, and I was discussing his fate with a friend.

"He ought to be sent to jail," said my friend. "He ought to be hung. Any man ought to be hung who doesn't know any better than to be right when all other decent healthy people in the world are wrong."

However, let me return to my theme. I am trying to sketch briefly some of the conditions that are at the bottom of what I conceive to be going on nowadays in American writing. When we Americans had got our country pretty well settled and had fought and won our Civil War, something else hap-

pened. There came a revolution more widespread and deep
in its meaning than any other revolution that has ever happened in the western world. Starting out as we did as an
agricultural people we Americans found ourselves suddenly
landed in the very midst of the industrial age. From being a
nation of farmers, craftsmen and merchants we became,
almost within a generation, the leading industrial nation of
the world. We became factory hands rather than craftsmen,
owners of factories rather than landowners.

We had got into a new age almost over night. What had
happened to us?

Standardization, for one thing.

Let me explain. As a natural result of industrial growth
came standardization. As anyone will understand, the man
who owns a factory for the making of women's dresses, chew-
ing gum, cigars, automobiles, men's hats, must, if his factory
is to grow to the huge output he desires, create in the public
mind a widespread demand for one kind of cigar, one kind of
hat, one style of dress, one make of automobile.

Advertising as a force in our American life began to grow
and here it is that the present day American writer came into
flower.

As a natural result of the demand for standardization of
taste and material desires came the modern magazine. The
magazine with a circulation of a million or two million
became not unusual. The real purpose, as everyone under-
stands, was to create through advertising, a nation-wide
demand for certain commodities. The magazines were business institutions run by business men with business ends in
view. They have served the purpose for which they were
created admirably and taken for what they are, that is to say
at bottom merely as propaganda instruments for business
expansion, no man can quarrel with them.

However, it happens you see, that the advertising medium, put out frankly as an advertising medium, cannot exist.
Although the modern man and woman of the streets has been
pretty effectually standardized as regards his hat, the cigarette he smokes, the automobile he drives, he cannot in reality
be standardized. Few of us will as yet order our wives from a

mail order house. Although in America and during the long
period during which we have all been so busy conquering the
mechanical world we have in general looked upon the poet
or the artist as rather a sissy, a nut, a man who had better be
brushed aside, we all have something of the poet and lover in
us. We cannot, at least not as yet, spend our hours of leisure
outside factory and office hours just looking at advertisements of factory products and becoming excited because some
man has performed the heroic feat of going from the city of
New York to San Francisco, getting there in twenty four
hours in an aeroplane—instead of taking four or five days on
a train, has found a machine that will get him there. We are
really interested in the man in the machine—not in the
machine itself.

Little thoughts leak in. We wonder why the man wanted
to go to San Francisco in such a hurry—what he thought
and felt as he rushed along—what he was up to. There are
all kinds of disturbing little fancies. Our minds will not
become standardized. They fly away from the machine to the
man. There remains a curious interest in one another. Young
men take girls on their arms and wander out at night into the
darkness. Young men become friends and spend nights walking and talking together. Nothing that gets settled remains
quite settled. When some of us become too old or tired to try
anymore to think or feel there is always youth coming on.
Even marriage doesn't settle things for us although for a long
time our novelists went on the assumption that it did.

We find ourselves having to be intrigued into the pages of
the magazines—and if the magazines are to retain the large
circulation they require to do their work of standardization
writers must be made to serve their purpose.

The commercialization of the art follows as a perfectly
natural result.

The popular writer is then just the man of talent who is
willing to sell his talent to the business man who publishes
the magazine or to the book publisher after large sales and
the more talented he is the better he gets paid. There is a job
to be done and he does it, keeping his eye always on the main
chance, that is to say on the great unthinking buying public.

His position is pretty secure. In America we are in the habit of thinking of the thing that succeeds as good, and therefore the man whose books sell by the hundreds of thousands is looked up to with respect. If success is the standard of measurement how can we do anything else?

It happens, however, that the arts are not democratic, never have been, and probably never will be. The ordinary standards of measurement do no quite work. We all have a vague feeling there is something very much wrong. There is.

Let us look at the situation a moment. If you are a man conducting a magazine that has a circulation of hundreds of thousands, or if you are a movie magnate owning a business in which there is a huge initial investment, you have to be pretty careful about treading on toes, do you not? Your readers or patrons must not be offended or driven away. You are appealing, must of necessity appeal, to a large number of people, and among any large number of people there will be Catholics, Protestants, Christian Scientists, believers in the Garden of Eden, Darwinians, suburban housewives in large numbers, Puritans, moralists, all kinds of people with all kinds of notions of the good and bad.

Very well then—if you are a writer intent on catching and holding the fancy of the crowd, you have got to have a technique. You have got to become the artful dodger, have got to invent or learn the trick of creating in the mind of your audience the sensations of terror, delight, amusement, suspense, without in any way actually touching the reality of lives.

At the county fairs back in Ohio when I was a boy there used to be kind of faker who went about with a machine. Into this machine he put a pound of sugar and started it going. It whirled about with great rapidity and produced a kind of cloud-like candy concoction that looked tremendously inviting. A pound of sugar would make a bushel of the stuff, but when you had brought a bag of it and put a whole handful into your mouth it melted away to nothing.

That is in reality the effect desired in the manufacture of any popular art. It is the effect produced in reality by all the successful men, by the realists who pretend to give you photographic reproductions of life itself, by the respectable fine writers of the more conservative magazines and publishing houses, as well as the men who fill the pages of the cheap adventure magazines, the men called by the magazine fraternity "the bunk shooters." You must seem to give a lot while really giving nothing. No one must be hurt. No one must be offended. No one must be made to think or feel. Keep it up and you will get rich.

To actually touch people's lives is the unforgivable sin. Both thinking and feeling are dangerous exercises, and besides, people do not like them.

You have got to get a special technique but if you are a writer and can do it successfully you will be mighty well paid. Why, there are any number of writers in America who receive from two or three or even five thousand dollars for single short stories and if they are lucky and also sell movie rights they often get two or three times that much. Writers of the popular sort often make incomes of bankers or brokers, live during the summer in villas in Maine or in the California Carmel Highlands, drive expensive motor cars, own yachts and have a simply splendid time apparently and never during a long lifetime make a single contribution to the art of writing or write anything that a living soul would ever think of reading after the writer has died or his temporary vogue has passed.

I hope you understand, however, that all this has nothing at all to do with the art of writing, that is to say in any sense in which real writers of the world, men who have cared something about their craft have always thought of it. These men have no more to do with the art of writing than the average American movie star has to do with the art of acting or the men who make the girls' heads you see on the covers of our American magazines have to do with the art of painting. It is all a kind of special thing. You live in San Francisco and write dialect stories concerning an imaginary kind of people who live in a Dutch settlement in the Pennsylvania hills, or you live in a New York hotel and write stories about cowboys or heroic lumberjacks. It is totally unnecessary to know life, and in fact it will be better for you to let life alone. Life, you

see, is a complex delicate thing. Anything may happen in life.
We all know that. People hardly ever do as we think they
should. There are no plot short stories in life. All the clever
tricks by which effects are to be got on the printed page are
in reality a selling out of ourselves. If it is your purpose to live
in a pasteboard world you have got to avoid storms. There is
always that huge, comfortable, self-satisfied American audience made up of all kinds of people with little prejudices,
hates and fears that must not be offended. To know men and
women to be in the least sympathetic with them in their
actual trials and struggles is a handicap. If it is your desire to
be that kind of writer, to grow rich and be successful by writing and if you have a natural talent that can be made to serve
your purpose, stay just as far away as possible from any real
thinking or feeling about actual men and women. Stay in the
pasteboard world. Believe in your heroic cowboys and lumberjacks. Go to the movies all you can. Read the magazines.
Go to the short story schools and learn the bag of tricks.
Spend your time thinking up plots for stories and never by
any chance let the plots grow naturally out of the lives and
the hopes, joys and the sufferings of the people you are writing
about. That is the road to success.

And now, men and women, I am afraid you will think me
an ill-natured fellow. I have spent so large a part of my
allotted time here in speaking of what in my opinion is tend-
ing to make writing in America so bad. It doesn't seem right.
I must remember that I am from Chicago—a highly cultured
center, surely—and that in Chicago we have a motto. Our
city mayor got it up several years ago, and for a year or two it
was plastered about everywhere on the walls and billboards of
the city. "Put away your hammer and get out your horn," it
said.

Now I shall try to do that.

There is, you see, a modern movement in America. We are
not so self-satisfied as we must often seem to strangers, to
men from foreign parts. We still walk about and talk things
over among ourselves. There is, if you are sensitive enough to
feel it, a wistful something in the air here. You will feel it in
any large crowd. At present the Modern Movement is per-

haps a groping ill-defined movement, but it exists. In painting there are a number of men who have stopped making pleasant enough drawings of the old swimming hole and the magazine cover lady, who have thrown overboard the tricks of realism and representation and the absorption in surface technique and who are trying to bring feeling and form back into painting. The same thing is going on in the writing of poetry. Architecture is freeing itself from imitation of dead impulses and is taking new life.

In prose the movement is expressing itself in a growing number of men who are really trying to be honest to the materials in which they work.

Let me explain what I mean by that, if I can.

I think you will all agree with me that in an older day in America, when a great majority of the men who worked in the crafts, the blacksmiths, silversmiths, shoemakers, harness makers, saddle makers, builders of vehicles, furniture, etc., worked in small shops, with a few apprentices to help, there was a feeling in the workman that later was pretty much destroyed.

The factory came and swept the individual workman aside and with him went much of the old workman's feeling toward tools and materials.

The workman in the Ford factory, for example, has nothing at all to do with his tools or the materials in which he works. His own individual feeling toward tools and materials is ruthlessly suppressed. Individual reaction to tools and materials is simply not wanted. What is wanted is a highly standardized product turned out at a low manufacturing cost.

The hand of standardization is laid upon the workman in the factories as I have tried to show you how it is being laid upon the workman in prose who wants also to live on the expensive scale of the banker or the broker.

I have tried to show you here that the popular magazines are but factories for efficient standardization of the minds of people for the purpose of serving the factories. I think they do not really pretend to be anything else.

I am bringing no personal accusation against the factory owner or the publishers of factory-made literature. They are business men and if I were a business man I would try to be a good one. I would try to make money. And anyway the individual factory owner or the individual owner or owners of a magazine with a circulation of hundreds of thousands has no more to do with the matter than have you and I. They also are caught in a trap. Present day conditions are but the natural result of our living in an industrial age. Until the impulse for vast production of second-rate goods and the tendency to be satisfied with second-rate art wears itself out or people grow tired of it, things will go on just as they are.

Back of it all, of course, lies the silly notion that people can get happiness out of success, out of making money, the silly notion that any man can be happy doing poor or sloppy work no matter how much temporary success or praise he may win.

You must bear in mind that the mass of people here in America are pretty much what the mass of people have always been in every other country in every age. That is to say, rather lazy minded, pretty immature. We are given to childish pretense, to pretending to be the thing we secretly admire rather than to go to all the trouble of being it. We accept what is given us. For most of us, I suspect, bad hurried cheap work doesn't matter too much. It is the craftsman really who suffers.

Now if you will consider with me what I have just said and will bear in mind that the manufacturer of stories for popular magazines has nothing at all to do with writing, and if you will also bear in mind that the writer is but the workman whose materials are human lives, you will get at what I am trying to say and will understand the attitude toward his work that the so called Modern is trying to take.

The individual impulse in men to do good work goes on. Men are arising everywhere who are trying to be true to the very complex materials they have to try to handle. In spite of standardization the individual impulses of men as workmen cannot quite be put down.

As I have gone about in the streets of American towns and cities I have noticed that even the Ford cannot escape the workman impulse. Boys buy second hand Fords and rebuild them into 'Bugs' and these 'Bugs' are often enough light, graceful and fine. Ugly lines have been cut away. Something altogether lacking in grace has been made graceful and it would be worthwhile if people could come to understand that the boy who does that is a craftsman following a carftsman's impulse and is more important to the community than a dozen manufacturers of cheap novels, little tame verses, or cheap magazine stories. He is meeting the aesthetic needs of his nature with the materials at hand, and a Cezanne, a Matisse, a Turgenieff or a Shakespeare could do no more than that. The artist is, after all, but the craftsman working more intensively in more complex and delicate materials.

The artist who works in stone, in color, sounds, words, building materials, and often in steel, as in the designing of bodies for some of the finer automobiles, is but the craftsman working on materials that are often elusive and difficult to handle and bringing into his work not only the skill of the craftsman but also the attempt at an expression of some need of his own inner being. That is the whole story.

The Modern Movement, then, seen from this point of view, is in reality an attempt on the part of the workman to get back into his own hands some control over the tools and materials of his craft. In certain fields it is very difficult. In the theater, for example, the artist, to work at all, has to have an expensive equipment. There is needed a large investment and money doesn't like to take chances. It is much safer when the theater wants to be artistic to run into Belasco realism, bring a Child's restaurant onto the stage or have a real automobile cross the stage at thirty miles an hour—something of that sort, some stunt, is safer when large sums of money have to be spent.

However, the workman in words or in color has a better chance. If, for example, I can make my living by going somewhere and delivering a dull sermon, something like this, to a lot of good natured patient people, or by working six months of the year in an advertising agency writing soap advertisements, I can perhaps save enough money to write, disregarding the magazines for another six months. I know one very

good modern painter who becomes a house painter when he
is broke, and one of America's finest poets works as a reporter
on a newspaper. In America, just now, it is not too hard for a
man to make a living, particularly if he is discreet enough not
to have children.

And then things are slowly getting better. In his "Life on
the Mississippi" Mark Twain said something to the effect
that the writer in the end always wrote what the public and
the editors wanted. "We often write what we think and feel
but in the end we scratch all out and give them what they
want," he said. I am not quoting exactly. You will find it in
the book. The fact is that it was pretty much true in Twain's
day and isn't quite so true now.

That the workman is a better and truer man when he is
given control of the tools and materials of his craft is being
found out. There is a small public growing up that has dis-
crimination enough to want good work. Honest books begin
to sell a little. Honest painting that isn't just pretty picture
making begins to sell. Puritanism, as such, is pretty well
licked. It cannot any longer so easily suppress books of artistic
merit because some housewife is afraid the morals of her
daughter, who has just come home from the movies or the
Follies, will be ruined by being told how babies happen to be
born. The force of the New England moralistic culture is
spent. Today in America any man of talent who writes a book
that is significant, a work of art, can get it published and there
will be critics to acclaim him. The real pioneering for the
better workmen has been done by men like Whitman and
Dreiser for the writers, and others like Stieglitz, Marin and
the critics Rosenfeld, Cheney and others for the painters.

If you want to do good work and can pick up a living in
some way, there will be people to recognize what you are
trying to do, and perhaps no man has a right to ask more
than that. There are ways to get moments of happiness out
of life other than by making money and being successful, and
the men who grind out second-rate flashy stories for the magazines have their bad moments. They are not really happy
men. It is no fun, believe me, to wake up in the middle of

the night and to realize that you have sold out your own craft.

For it is as true as there is a sun in the sky that men cannot live in the end without love of craft. It is to the man what love of children is to the woman. When you are considering what it is that makes the younger generation so restless, what makes the workers on your buildings and in your factories such indifferent workmen, what makes so much of contemporary art cheap and transitory, consider also what the industrial age has tended to do to this old love of craft so deeply rooted in men.

It is a dangerous process. Soil the workman's tools and materials long enough and he may turn and kill you. You are striking at the very root of the man's being.

However, I do not want to be sensational. In spite of the growth of standardization there are for me many hopeful signs. Men are becoming increasingly conscious of what is being done to them. The very man who lends his talents to cheapness is unconvinced. He will come to you in private with an apology. "I have to live," he will say. "I have a wife and children. I am only doing cheap work for the time being. When I have made a little money I intend to do some honest, decent work."

In reality I think many men of talent might be saved for the doing of good work in the arts if the whole situation could be clearly stated. Too often the younger man or woman who has talent does not get the situation in hand until he is too old to save himself. We have all been brought up with the notion, firmly planted in us, that to succeed in a material sense is the highest end for a life. Our fathers tell us that. Often our mothers tell us so. Schools and universities often enough teach the same lesson. We hear it on all sides and when we are young and uncertain our very youthful humbleness often enough betrays us. Are we to set ourselves up against the opinions of our elders? How are we to know that truth to ourselves, to the work of our own hands, to our own inner impulses, is the most vital thing in life? It has become almost a truism here in America that no man does good work in the arts until he is past forty. Nearly all the so called Moderns, the younger men, so called, are already gray. It takes a long time for most men to get ground under their feet, to find out a little their own truth in life.

The effort to find out the truth is what is called the Modern Movement. It is growing. Do not have any doubt about that.

Let me state the matter again. It cannot be stated too often. The writer, the painter, the musician, the practitioner of any of the arts who wants to do real work and honest work, has got to put money making aside. He has got to forget it. There is but one way in which the young man or woman of talent can defeat the corrupting influence of the present day magazines and most of the book publishers, and that is by forgetting their existence and giving all his attention to his work. And again let me say that when I speak of corrupting influence I am not speaking of the men who run these institutions as corrupt individuals. I am speaking only in the workman's sense. I am speaking only of the workman in relation to his tools and materials.

Consider for a moment the materials of the prose writer, the teller of tales. His materials are human lives. To him these figures of his fancy, these people who live in his fancy, should be as real as living people. He should be no more ready to sell them out than he would sell out his men friends or the woman he loves. To take the lives of these people and bend or twist them to suit the needs of some cleverly thought out plot to give your readers a false emotion is as mean and ignoable as to sell out living men or women. For the writer there is no escape, as there is no real escape for any craftsman. If you handle your materials in a cheap way you become cheap. The need of making a living may serve as an excuse but it will not save you as a craftsman. Nothing really will save you if you go cheap with tools and materials. Do cheap work and you yourself are cheap. That is the truth.

To speak again of the way out for the Moderns—for the young man or the young woman who wishes to do work for which he need not, in the end and when the temporary acclaim that so often follows cheap and flashy work has passed, be ashamed, well, there is one. In America it is not too difficult to make a living. Mr. Henry Mencken says that in America any man not a complete fool cannot help making a living, and there is some truth in what he says. If you have no money and no one will give you any, make your living in some other way and keep the real side of yourself for the honest work you want to do in your own craft. There are worse fates than being poor. If you have talent do not sell out your birthright. My own belief is that there never was a people in the world more anxious for men of talent to stay on the track and be true to the crafts then we Americans. We all know something is wrong with the flood of cheap work we are always getting. The literary clubs and the various kinds of culture clubs that spring up everywhere are perhaps rather silly in some of their gropings, but they mean something. Often enough the man who spends all his own life absorbed in money making would really like his wife and children to have something else as an end in life. I suspect that is the real reason there are so many young men and women in colleges who have no real interest in scholarship. They want something and their parents want something for them. Is it any wonder they do not know what they want?

At bottom, Americans are kind. They are good natured. So anxious are we as a people for men of talent that it takes but the merest show of talent to get recognition among us. Why, any man or woman who wants to be respected has but to set himself up as a poet. He does not need to write poetry. Let him write a few verses. We will all invite to dine with us, we will put up with his idiosyncrasies and small vanities, we will nurse and feed him like a very babe.

And if he is a musician or a young painter we will, as likely as not, shell out our money and send him off to Paris to become as commonplace and unreal and successful as an artist as the very people we have been talking about here today.

But my preaching on this subject had better come to an end. It is a subject on which books might be written. When your young man or woman has made the sacrifices for the sake of a craft that I have spoken of as necessary—and they are not really sacrifices at all—the struggle has but begun. There remains the question of talent and if you have talent that doesn't settle the matter.

There is no agreement among artists as to the ends they are seeking, no absolute standards. "A.E.", the famous Irish publicist, painter and poet, once said that a literary movement consisted of several men of talent living at the same time and cordially hating each other.

That is the truth and yet it is not quite true. What it really means is that when men are devoted to their work there will still remain a wide difference of opinion as to methods, treatments of the subject, the baffling question of form achieved or not achieved—the question of when a craftsman's work becomes also a work of art. These are old questions about which all craftsmen have always struggled among themselves. It is all a queer and fascinating game, just as life itself is queer and fascinating.

The real reward, I fancy, lies just in the work itself, nowhere else. If you cannot get it there, you will not get it at all.

And speaking for my craft I can say that it is tremendously worth while. You are undertaking a task that can never be finished. You are starting on a road that has no end. The longest life will be too short to ever really get you anywhere near what you want. And that I should say is the best part of the story.

LETTERS FROM SHERWOOD ANDERSON

(circa 1931-1936)

Dear Etta Stetheimer:[1]

I'm sorry I did not get in to see you before I left New York. I wasn't well, wasn't working and came home expecting to return to New York before finally coming for the summer but simply stayed here. Mrs. Anderson coming later.

We have been having guests. There is held here annually what they call a musical festival. It is held on one of the highest mountains east of the Mississippi, a mountain only some twenty miles from our house.

The idea is that the mountaineers, men and women, will come trooping up into the mountain. They will burst into song. There is a kind of man or woman who goes in heavy for FOLK . . . Percy McKaye and others. They all come.

They have had a good deal of trouble. Young men from New York's east side put on faded overalls, tie red handkerchiefs on their neck and get all the prizes. Some of these New York east siders usually get washed up on our doorsteps. It is wonderful. Two or three years ago Mrs. Roosevelt was here. There must have been at least ten thousand people that year all searching the lonely mountain singer.

You should come down and see us here. The country is very beautiful.

I hear from Paul Rosenfeld that you have moved. Lewis Galantiere[2] was here with his tall beautiful wife. Ferdinand Schevill[3] is coming in September and perhaps, if he can get away from his Virgin Islands then Robert Lovett[4] will come.

I am writing only short stories. I have a lot I want to tell if I can.

I would like news of you.

Roger Sergel

Dear Roger:

You mustn't be tired, old dear, and that's what your letter a little sounds like. Read Edmund Wilson's new book.

---

[1] Writer, sister of Florine Stetheimer, famous artist.
[2] Author.
[3] Professor of History, Univ. of Chicago.
[4] Professor of English, Univ. of Chicago.

Not that this has anything to do with tiredness but I do think Wilson manages to give out of himself to all of us.

About the play, I have for the time forgotten it.

Paul's new book is good.

As usual I have many things to talk of with you but there you are and here I am.

Of a sudden for some unknown reason my stories begin to sell in England. I did a new short story and a profile of Jasper Deeter[1] for the NEW YORKER.

As regards this matter of suggestion. Why Roger I don't suppose any man working in the arts really takes them. He has to remain if he can in a certain receptive mood. As you well know, an incident in a restaurant or something seen in the street may influence him more than anything any of his comrades may say.

That doesn't mean that the rubbing of mind against mind isn't good.

Between ourselves I have given up the Civil War idea also the idea that I can take financial aid from Mary Emmett[2].

I don't know why but it won't work.

And perhaps the continual struggle for leisure to work and live, always a bit on the edge, is better.

I've been a little ill but I'm better now. I wonder if I'd better ask you to send the cut or bring it. I think I'd better wait and have you bring it. It may be the best way to insure that you two are actually coming.

Dear Roger:

As for the daily newspapermen—in criticism, how can they be other than they are? Imagine trying to review a book a day—Great God! Do you wonder they are book weary— snatch at old ideas? The big Sundays, like the Herald and Times here, escape this weariness by assigning books to quite a big list of reviewers.

Had a note from Max Perkins this morning. He says that

---

[1] Jasper Deeter, Founder of the Hedgerow Theatre, Rose Valley, Pa.
[2] Wife of Burton Emmett, advertising executive and print collector.

the day when you can go out and load the book stores with big advance sales, is over—to quote, "We have ordered second printing. The books seems to us to be getting off about as most of these successes now do."

I suspect these printings are not large.

Roger—I suspect that you're tired of hearing of Kit. I am, rather, myself. And also I guess the News reviewer may be right that I have got to some sort of maturity as the reviewers, say like, Fadiman, do not bother me at all.

There are amusing angles. A magazine called "Mid-Week Pictorial", had a review that suggested I must have written with the movies in mind and, George Nathan, who is enthusiastic about the book told me that it was movie sure-fire. So, you see, I may be getting an offer and if I do I will take it, not, of course, going near their damned Hollywood.

Oh, I get your slant O.K. But, Roger, we do not have much criticism such as you could do. I wouldn't want you to be in a position of having to do reviews of books at any stated time and, it may be, that reviewing books is not what I have in mind.

The point is that you have that very rare thing among men who write of writing, a mind. You know something of what it's all about. It wouldn't hurt you, old darling, to sit down now and then and do a piece.

And as for that, I'm going to keep sticking the idea in here and there, until anyway there's a place.

Can't work any long thing here. I did this week a kinda swell thing on the Brown Bomber—Joe Louis; after seeing him fight the other night.

Here's a drink to the new house.

S.A.

P.S. Drop a little note to North and tell him how you feel. I wrote him.

Nyack, N.Y.

Monday

Dear Roger

I am in the country, in a very lovely place, Mary Emmett's farm, on The Hudson, about thirty miles above New York.

I'm working here. It was good good to hear from you.

I finished the first writing of the Novel . . . "Kit Brandon" and am at work revising.

Also I have got the new play down to the last two scenes. By the way I am wondering about something. I'd rather like to do a book . . . Scribners . . . The Winesburg, the new play . . . present title "They Shall Be Free" and the short stories. The Triumph of The Egg . . . A short play called "Mother" and one yet unfinished. What sort of deal could I make with you for the releasing of Triumph, to appear in the book?

I have a rather gaudy play. As you know my friend, Burton Emmett, advertising man, died recently. Both E and I are very fond of Mary, his wife, who is quite rich. Since I have been a kid I have wanted to do a long history of the Civil War and now Mary has proposed that she will give me the money to do it . . . it to be a kind of memorial to Bert. I think I'll do it. I'm asking E to quit her job and the present plan is to go to Washington, after Christmas to work until summer in the Congressional Library. Doesn't it sound gaudy. It's wonderful to have this big hard job ahead.

I wonder what you'll think of the novel. Its more outside me and impersonal than anything else I've done. I do think that perhaps I have created a rather nice, hard-boiled but yet very decent woman.

But that's enough of me. E is quite well . . . as I am. I work steadily. I see no chance now for coming to New York but perhaps you'll be down here in November. We'll be at 54 Washington Mews.

Lots of love to Ruth and the lads
S.A.

Fall 1935

Charles Bockler[1]

Sept. 17, 1931
Roanoke, Va.

Dear Charles:

I have a feeling of guilt for not having written before. I am in Roanoke today and will not return to Marion before

---

[1] Baltimore artist.

morning. It is hot. I have been wandering in the woods a good deal this summer and just now my hands and arms are covered with poison ivy.

John came and last Sunday we had a few hours together looking at his paintings. There is a big advance. We both agree that being with you had done something fine to his work this summer.

I could feel your color influence. There was, I thought, both a new boldness and a new delicacy. All of John's relationship with you has been good for him as a person and as a painter.

I have published a little book. I don't know how it will be received. In a few days, when I have copies, I will send one to you.

The big thing on which I have been at work a long time goes slowly. It is hard to orchestrate it.

Maurice Long was down here and spoke again of what your still life had done to his house. It is in the living room— a long, low room—over the mantle.

The walls are light brown and there is a panelling of grained wood in darker color. The painting seems to throb and live there.

He wants another of your things. If you have one for him —something you like—tell me and you can send it on to him. Also tell me what he should pay for it.

The husband of that Mrs. Wilson who came to see your things in Baltimore is in Marion and came into our apartment. He saw the little watercolor I have—the one of red houses amid trees. It is done in blocks of color—different from any other of your things I have seen. He talks of buying it. May I let him have it? How much should I ask for it?

I am sorry you are perhaps rather discouraged, Charles—if you are. I myself have had little to give. You must have felt it. I fight all the time against a kind of deadness in people now. It may be in me.

Lately I have been better. I have been trying to save—or sing—something new about the machine. If some day we are to have a new civilization—based on Communism—some form of it—and I think we are—it will have to be based on the machine.

I am trying a little to project myself into the new life, now having the theory that the new life is already here and only doesn't yet become in any sense beautiful because we don't accept it. Lot of luck.

Feb. 12, 1933
Kansas City, Mo.

Dear Charles and Kack:[2]

I think my first impulse—in coming out here—to a middle western city in the winter was to get away from small town life for a time—hear again the fire wagon scream, street cars jangle—mingle with middle western crowds on the streets at night. I have got a large work room, with bedroom adjoining, 2 baths, 2 closets, for 1 dollar per day in a hotel—and right in the heart of the city. Food is much cheaper now too. The street, full of people and of work. Street prostitution springing up again. I came out in my little car.

I sent home and had Bob send me, by express, one of your paintings—the one of green treetops—I always loved a still life of John's soft rich velvety color. Also I have a new and nice Lankes print.

I was getting out a book of short stories and it had gone to the printer but I wasn't satisfied—so I wrote a new short story—about 7 or 8,000 words—called *"Brother Death."* I think you'll like it.

It got down to 25 below and I had flu—cursing and cursing until it passed. I am in a new novel I'm calling *"Thanksgiving"*—written in the mood rather of *"A Story Teller's Story."* It is so far loose and fluid. I had some twenty years in offices of advertising agencies being a little whore there—and never used the material. I had had too much hatred. Now perhaps at last I am far enough away from it to use it. We'll see.

(This seems to be a letter full of me and my doings. Well, it can't be helped. I'm in that mood I guess.)

I've decided to go back to Ripshin Farm. There the farm is—with a big stone house all furnished and I can't sell it.

---

[2] His wife.

I guess I got jammed up there because of the woman I was living with—not her fault—not the right chemical mixture perhaps . . .

Afterwards—the feeling about the place—my failure there. It is passed now.

I have been reading *"The Letters of D. H. Lawrence."* Would you like to see them? If you would, write and I'll send them—but would like them back later.

I've a sort of an idea—to try to build up—at Ripshin—a place where a few men can come to work if they want to. They can put up shacks or tents, as they please. We might— I'd say not over three or four men with their women share expense—a common dining room . . . no one tied down to it. Do you think such things can ever work?

Bob wrote John had come down there. Perhaps he's there now. I like his work and his tone more and more.

Write and tell me how things go with you and Kack,

S.A.

P.S. Yesterday—on the street I was panhandled by a young man—23 he told me—a young man with a very sensitive face. I gave him something and said—"Come on let's walk and talk a little." He told me that he had walked all the night before—no money for a bed—zero weather. His eyes were bloodshot and there was something—that curious dirtiness and messiness that comes of never changing your clothes— sleeping in them etc. So as we walked I asked him—"Why don't you tie up with the Reds?" He looked at me with sus- picion and then decided I was O.K. but said he believed in individualism. "I'd rather be a lone wolf even if I starve," he said. "I might beat the game yet."

Rugged individualism—you see. It will apparently be a long time before Americans—even the down and outs—real- ize that individualism of that sort has only come to mean, crawling up over someone else. Page Jesus Christ.

Dear Charles . . .

I have been thinking of you a great deal lately. It may be because of the fall and because I am in the country where the colors change from day to day. I have a little room in a house in the country, an hour by car from New York, on the Hudson, and my typewriter desk, as I sit at work, faces a window that looks out across a small lake.

In the forefront an orchard, the trees, most of them quite bare now. There is one to which bright yellow leaves still cling, a few yellow apples in the dry grey grass, a pile of fence rails, soft grey against one of the trees. There is a road in the distance that cars go along, and I like that. Also, across the little lake, hills . . . after the leaves go a feeling of the bones of the earth, nice and firm. Behind the hills is the Hudson.

I went and bought Van Gogh's letters. They also made me think of you. I want John to have them. They cost $22.50 but are well worth it.

But I must tell you how I got here. That Mary Emmett, whose husband Bert was one of the men who bought one of your paintings, that time we got up $500, died in the early summer. In the fall, when I was still at Ripshin and when Eleanor had to leave and come to N.Y., she came down to take care of me. Afterwards we came up here, to her farm. I wouldn't be surprised if, in the future, she more or less lived with E and me and we with her. She is lonely and has no children, a peculiarly vigorous woman of sixty who loves working out of doors, etc. She has money and no pretentions, and wants affection and companionship, and is willing to help me accomplish some things I have been dreaming of doing, and that will bring no money.

Are you working . . . I mean regularly employed? I thought it possible that, before Christmas, I would get John to come up here for perhaps a week. I spoke to Mary Emmett of this and she suggested that if you could come for a week, perhaps at the same time, she would pay your expenses. I thought you and John could take a room together perhaps and go about seeing things. Write me if you think it possible . . . at 54 Washington Mews, and then we will try to work it out about the time, etc.

I am working hard. Give my regards to Kack. Tell her not to take my letter too seriously as I do not hers. As always

Sherwood

Fall 1935

*Karl Anderson**

Sept. 16, 1931
Marion, Va.

Dear Karl:

I feel cruel—leaving that on you. I'm afraid it would be unendurable to me. It must be happening everywhere. These members of families that could just adjust thrown back on families. But why should it be you? It may be because you are a propertied man, with a house you live in. Somewhere to go. They always sell insurance.

I'm afraid my new book isn't going to strike. They may not be ready for it and then, again, it may not say it clearly and strongly enough.

At least I have made the choice—to go with the machine— not to reject it anymore.

It is going to be a cruel time, I'm afraid. When society tries to adjust itself it does it always with such cruel slow movements. Children walking in bitterness. God help us all.

I remember that fat little man. He was terribly naive and gabby. It was impossible not to know that he couldn't make it no matter how he tried.

He should have been a factory hand. There isn't enough craft in him to make it go in a horsetrading world. At least he might have served under Mr. Ford.

It may be true of me too. I've often wished I had stayed where I began—an ordinary worker. I might, at least, have been a voice coming up out of that period.

I am happy about the novel. It sounded good to me that day when I sat in that funny empty hotel dining room with you. I'd go with one of the larger publishers in N.Y.—Macmillan, or Harper's or Scribners or Liveright. Liveright would be eager to see the book if you felt like going there. They have been square, I think, with me.

I keep trying to organize my own novel—by some new road to me. Hardly a personal story. I would like the machine

* His elder brother.

ripping up and down through it, the distracted workers—
men and women being beaten and killed as the world tries to
adjust itself—as men try to struggle with a new world. I
daresay I'll never get what I hope for.

I have this ever present feeling nowdays that the whole
world is in a queer birth time. This weariness always in us.
What does it come from? We might be quite jolly old men
marching forward to death. Surely death is a house.

Nothing is changed in nature. I walk out or ride out here
and the corn comes up out of the ground. Nature is a great
poem—singing, cruel, smiling and real. Always a woman—
Hanson says, in substance, of me. It is only nature. I feel it
more deeply in women, acceptance, joy of contact etc. It has
never been just the senses. Any woman knows that of me.

To return to Ray. I don't know what to say. There isn't
anything here. John has come here to work the winter with
Bob in the printshop. I'll have to travel and lecture this
winter so I'll be in New York and see you. Bob is going to
marry. John has painted all this summer. When Bob marries
I'll give up ½ of the little apartment here and live in a room.
I half hoped to go to Russia next year, to see what I can feel
there. Are they getting hold of life again? Is there hope and
life there? I'd give much to know. I'll be sending you the
book. Love

Sherwood

Will Alexander*

Dear Will Alexander:

I sit down to write you this morning. I think I told you
how I stumbled into this field. I had come down here into
the hills of Southwest Virginia to live, having somewhat a
hunger for life with a southern atmosphere and also for life
in the smaller American communities.

When I had been here for some time I bought the only
two weekly newspapers in the county. It was a fairly well

---

* Southern Sociologist—a dignitary in the Rosenwald Foundation.

equipped plant, with a five thousand dollar lin-o-type machine, sufficient fonts of type, a job printing outfit, flat bed press and folder . . . a good enough little shop.

I go into such details a little because it has a bearing on what I want to say.

I paid $15,000 for the plant and assumed about $3,000 in debts. Of this I borrowed $4,000 at a bank here, gave the man $7,000 in notes, and put in $4,000 of my own.

That was just three years ago. All has been paid off except $2500 at the bank, and we have bought about $2000 in new equipment.

To do this I have taken nothing from the business myself, but have paid the salary of another editor and a reporter and have raised the salaries of the workmen about $25 a month each.

I got into this matter for these reasons. I was living in this community. The town of Marion, the county seat, has about 4,000 people. There are several smaller towns in the county, the county having about 25,000 people.

The two papers in the county were owned by one man. I think a somewhat typical smalltown publisher nowadays. He ran the papers merely as moneymaking institutions, tried to squeeze out all he could, putting in as little as possible. He was afraid of the politicians, of the churches, of almost everyone. The papers had a yearly subscription price of $1.25 per year. Hardly anyone paid for his paper. There were people on the books, we found out after taking charge, who had been receiving the papers for ten years, having paid nothing.

There were two papers; one is Democratic and the other Republican. When I bought them, this afforded a good deal of amusement to people outside. Anderson was to write with a Republican right hand and a Democratic left hand, some of the city dailies said.

As a matter of fact it was very simple to handle. I turned the political page, that is to say that portion of it devoted to politics, over to two men appointed by the two political parties, giving equal space to each, not censoring anything they wrote, paying them no salaries. I reserved the right to censor or reject all editorials on local affairs, not political.

I wrote no political editorials myself.

These men, during political campaigns, also sent in political news items regarding meetings, etc. These I published, giving the Republicans the use of the Republican paper for Republican announcements, claims, etc., and the same for the Democrats with the Democratic paper.

Incidentally, as I found out, there was a game on in the county. The county happens to be one of the few in the state that has usually a Republican majority. It is a mountain county with three rich farming valleys. The hill men incline to be Republicans, a hangover in Virginia of the Civil War and Reconstruction. East Tennessee and this section of Virginia sent a good many men into the Northern army. The Republican politicians had made some sort of deal with the publisher. The Republican paper, called "The Smyth County News", was an eight page paper, the Democratic paper was about four pages. Every effort was made to throw subscribers to the Republican paper. There was talk among the Democrats of starting a paper of their own. I made both papers the same size. I announced the policy of making all subscribers pay in advance. I raised the subscription prices from $1.25 a year to $1.75.

You must forgive me, Alexander, for all these details. I will get at my picture soon.

Incidentally, the raising of the subscription price I felt necessary to carry the load. I had to make them want the papers. I had to make the advertisers want to advertise. I succeeded in doing both of these things after a struggle. A good many said it was because I was Sherwood Anderson, because the New York Times sent a reporter to interview me about the enterprise, etc., but it is not true. Not three people in the county had ever heard of me. A story got out about that I wrote books and an old mountain man came in to see me. "I hear you write books," he said. "We want you to make a go of it here but don't depend on selling us books. We don't buy no books. A good many of us can't read. I have to get my daughter to read the weekly paper to me. We can't fool with no books."

When I had got cleared away I do not believe we had a

thousand subscribers on the two papers. We still get $1.75 a
year in advance but our plan is presently to chop the price
to $1.00 a year. We go rapidly toward 4,000 readers. With
a subscription price of $1.00 I am sure we can double it.

I am sending you, attached, a few typical issues of the
papers now. I have got also a book out of the experience. I am
sending a copy of that.

*   *   *

INFLUENCE OF THE WEEKLIES

There are 2500 people in this county. About 300 copies of
dailies come in. The daily is dead after one day. The weekly
is handed about from neighbor to neighbor. Subscribers, after
reading, mail it to relatives.

It should be born in mind that these weeklies are not newspapers in the daily sense. All of this is rather outlined in an
article prepared for magazine publication attached.

The secret of success with country weeklies is to keep the
papers local in a news sense. We have a correspondent at
every crossroads in the county; often the schoolteacher. We
tell everyone in the county about people's small doings, when
they kill hogs, begin planting corn, go visiting, etc. State and
national news and all foreign news is terrifically condensed,
about a column a week. We try to keep the papers down
where the people live.

The opportunity for using these papers lies in going constantly to the people. Your country editor has columns of
space to fill. Most country editors fill space with cheap plate
matter bought at a low price. It is more economical than setting type, even on a linotype. Cheap stories, propaganda put
out by commercial companies, banker's organizations, etc.,
fill them up. You can get this stuff free . . . all you want of it.

We have tried publishing some of the best stories and
articles in old literature. The readers have liked it. We didn't
tell them it was highbrow stuff to scare them off.

There are a thousand ways in which the influence of these
country papers could be increased. There could be no better

way to get after better county government, check brutalities, give voice to the better influences already in the country. It is a job for women as well as men.

In our county we have made several fights. The county jail was a filthy, unsanitary hole. After a year's pounding, we got through a bond issue, and have now a decent sanitary jail.

We built a small town park. This we offered to do at our own expense if the town would furnish the ground. The town did. It cost us nothing. People came from all over the county bringing shrubs, bulbs, etc. There was some filling to do. The dirt was furnished free.

There was no library here. We opened a renting library in the print shop and have now more than a thousand volumes. People pay $1.50 to join the library and 15¢ a week when they take out a book. If they move out of town the $1.50 is returned, (they always apply it on next year's paper). The library is non-profit making. All the money goes to buy more books.

We have made a fight for a new colored school. Last year we almost had it. The colored mechanics of the town offered to build the school, doing their work free if the town would furnish site and material. It would have gone through but a colored preacher, a rather self-assertive man, antagonized a lot of people and spoiled things. Now the county superintendent of schools has had the matter up with the Rosenwald Fund and things look encouraging. The present colored school is a disgrace to the county. We have tried, without scolding, to make the people feel this.

The above are things—definitely accomplishments. We would never claim any credit for them here but I think we are given credit throughout the county. The real influence such a paper can expect is hard to get at. Much may be done by subtle little thrusts, articles, talks, etc. People write letters to the paper. We get others to reply. What is aimed at is a broader point of view, less local hatreds, more humanity, building community pride, etc. I think you yourself, Mr. Alexander, have told me how difficult it is to reach the country editors for your own inter-racial propaganda. It is because the county weeklies are so often now in small money-grubbing hands.

A PROBLEM

We had here for example an amusing problem. This is a mountain country. There are a good many makers of moon whiskey in the hills. This stuff is brought to town and sold. Formerly, when such a man was caught by the sheriff and brought into court, or if a workman, or a negro had bought the stuff and was taken up, there would be an account of it in the paper. But, if the son of one of our first families got drunk, smashed an automobile, etc., not a word appeared.

In Virginia, family is everything. Certain families have considered themselves sacred. Soon after we came here the son of one of the first families of Virginia . . . an F. F. V. . . . got into trouble, and we published the story as though he had been a working man or a farmer. It fairly stood the county on its head. It was the best thing we did. It made us liked back in the hills and valleys and in the houses of the town factory workers.

* * *

MY DREAM

I have spoken to you, Mr. Alexander, of what I would like to do. I would like to devote myself to increasing the number of first class men and women going into this field. I remember that when I came here I wrote, for Outlook magazine, an article called "Nearer the Grass Roots." The phrase expresses something.

There are so many people in the country in small towns who never take a daily. These people have feelings too. They are what Abraham Lincoln called, the Common People. Unfortunately, as you know, and particularly in the South, among the poor whites, there have been long generations of these people being brutalized. They are the leftovers of the hatred brought on by slavery, race prejudices, the appeals of cheap politicians, etc.

Everything cannot be done at once, but you can see the possible effect of having the country weeklies these people read in better hands. What I want to see done now is a start made at organized propaganda to bring this about. This kept up for say the next ten years to bring the right kind of young men and women into this field.

There should be work done in the schools and colleges. Particularly in the South there are, as everyone knows, too many young lawyers and doctors. Everywhere are young men and women who have, at least while young, an impulse to serve.

Personally, I think it could be made a field for the development of new leadership in politics, in literature, in civilization. I dream of seeing, in every southern state, twenty to thirty, possibly a hundred really live country editors, instead of two or three, as at present. I dream of seeing them fighting ugly prejudices, mass brutality, stupidity.

*   *   *

THE EDITOR'S VIEWPOINT

I think you will grant me, Mr. Alexander, that there is already some reaction in the country away from the impulse for just bigness. There is, at least, the beginning of what is called "an agrarian movement." In the attached article I have said something about the cramping effect of present day big newspaper work on young men and women.

The editor is in a much more powerful position in the community than the preacher, the lawyer, the doctor. His power could be almost unlimited. He has his audience always before him. If he can be patient, a little courageous and good natured, he can bring the politicians to time, make them be decent. He can fight the brutalizing influences in the community life and back the influences that stand for decency.

There is needed a center of propaganda for the movement. An effort should be made to make it a movement. There should be a central office established, and well organized propaganda to show young men and women the possibilities of this field.

I have myself done what I can in this matter. Already a good many young men write to me. Some man should begin going about and lecturing on the subject in schools and colleges calling attention to the country newspaper field as a possibility.

Those who are already in should be encouraged. It is rather discouraging now, Mr. Alexander, to go to a state meeting of these country editors. As you will see by the attached article on this subject, I believe that the country papers have in so many cases got into the hands of second rate men because of the cityward movement that has for so long a time drained off the brighter young men and women.

There are however, good men and women already in the field, and they like the work.

However, they feel isolated. They should be brought together in some sort of spiritual sense. I myself think two things should be done. First, serious and sustained work carried on to get better men and women into the field, raising its tone, and then all the men and women now in made to feel they are a part of something.

The whole thing should be built on broad cultural lines as, force for decency; a possible force for decency being developed.

*Laura Lou Copenhaver**

Dear Mother . . .

E will be here tomorrow, in time for dinner and I am glad. It is quite terrible. I find myself more and more needing her every day. She writes me that Mary has got a new Packard and is driving east. If you really feel you want her to pay you a visit you could wire her c/o H. Kelly Pratt, at Gaylord, Kans. E says she has been so busy she has had no time to write. I have been getting short, but cryptic notes from her.

* His mother in law.

Jap is to have a reading of the play to the company. We will wait for that. If they decide to do it this year we will go ahead with the copying. If you have gone ahead, O.K. I feel the play is better theatre. Whether or not it is as close to life as Winesburg is another matter. Winesburg, with the new setting, goes back into the repertoire next month. They keep getting demands for it. I have begun the first scene of the comedy about which I wrote you but am also working on a long short story, about a ball player and two women.

A letter from Perkins of Scribners about Kit. He says, "Extremely interesting, exciting and significant. It tells so much about America. It has plenty of the proletariat angle in it and much more rightly than the proletarians give it. It makes you realize what a strange country America now is." From which, mother, I take it that he is pleased with us.

Lots of love
S.A.

Spring 1936

Wed. 54 Washington Mews   N.Y.

Dear Mother:

As you see we are in New York. Mary is up at her farm, planting her garden. We are going back over to Hedgerow on Friday and E will come back here Sunday night.

I think I'll go for a week to Washington, returning to Hedgerow for the next week end and again meeting E there. That will bring me up to May 24th. Then another little visit to New York and home. Mary may come down with me. E can't leave New York until June 11th. I'll see Mazy[1] and Channing[2] on the Washington trip.

The new act written into the play changes it some. I may send the new version to be copied entire. I read the new act to Jap and he agrees with me about it. It brings Tom and his wife Kate a bit closer in the end . . . that is to say "man and

---

[1] Mrs. Channing Wilson, sister in law of S. A.
[2] Channing Wilson, brother in law of S. A.

woman." E and I are to go to cocktails with Perkins of Scribners tomorrow. I already have one inquiry about the play from a big producer here . . . he evidently having heard there was a new one. It is interesting how closely these N.Y. producers watch Jap. I am trying to work out a project that might give them the summer season here and the winter season in New Orleans.

E is looking fine. Do you know I believe she and I are falling in love with each other. How very unromantic.

Lots of love to all there.
S.A.

Spring 1936

Dear Mother . . .

I knew the idea of my going to Columbia would excite you . . . having a son-in-law a professor, instead of that annoying and so often irritating thing, an artist. Confess it.

But alas, it may not turn out. The suggestion came, it's true, from a department head, as a question . . . would I consider it? No definite offer has been made and I may well hear no more about it. I presume any such thing would have to be approved up above. So we had better not count on that.

I have accepted an offer to go speak in Chicago in January.

As for the young Southern boy, when the part of the book you have is copied and you run through it you will see that I have not yet come to him. Yes, I do think your suggestions good ones. I do intend to develop that relationship for the very purpose you have in mind.

E sent the story, "Playthings" to Vanity Fair. If it comes back I will send it down to you at once.

I have had a flare up of the sinus, very unpleasant, but it hasn't yet stopped me from working.

S.A.

Lots of love to all.
Weather cold and wet now.

Friday

Dear Mother . . .

A cool clear morning. I am to write you specially about a particular matter. Last evening E and I went for a cocktail with Mr. Maxwell Perkins. He fell for E and she for him. He is so perfectly the gentle man . . . not gentleman . . . He talked of the novel.

A matter came up. Before we left for the west I sent him the first part of the novel. E says that, later, when I got out west, I began and rewrote it all. I do not think so. I think I rewrote only the latter half.

At any rate he says the book was sent to him in the two pieces and that they overlapped. He can straighten it out but E is of the impression that there is a complete copy there, in the files. Do you mind looking? If you find such a complete copy will you send it on to Eleanor and she will take it to Perkins.

We are leaving for Hedgerow this P.M. but E will be back in New York on Monday. I am going to Washington and will stop to see Mazy and Channing. I want to visit John and see some people in Washington. Will be back at Hedgerow the following week-end.

Tell May I got her grand letter and am tickled that everything went well at Ripshin. I begin to hunger very much to see you all.

With Love
S.A.

Spring 1936